FRESH & FAST:
MEALS FROM THE OVEN

FRESH & FAST: MEALS FROM THE OVEN

Annette Yates and Norma Miller

RIGHT WAY

Typeset in 10 pt Swiss 721 by Letterpart Ltd., Reigate, Surrey.

Printed and bound in Great Britain by Cox & Wyman Ltd., Reading, Berkshire.

The *Right Way* series is published by Elliot Right Way Books, Brighton Road, Lower Kingswood, Tadworth, Surrey, KT20 6TD, U.K. For information about our company and the other books we publish, visit our website at www.right-way.co.uk

CONTENTS

INTRODUCTION

Do you long for some delicious, real, home-prepared food cooked in the oven, but because of your busy modern lifestyle you never find the time? If so, the recipes in this book will show you how to make your oven work to your advantage.

All the recipes are fast to prepare, but the cooking times vary from 10 minutes to 24 hours. This makes them ideal for all situations and occasions. The shorter ones can easily be prepared, cooked and served on a weekday evening at the end of a busy day, just what you or your family might need to revive flagging energy. The recipes with the longer, slower cooking times are ideal for family or friends at weekends or holidays. On these days you might have plenty to do, but you can often separate the food preparation from the meal time by a couple of hours or more. Quickly put the dish together, and after placing it in the oven, turn your mind to other things. Sit back and relax with a glass of wine and listen to some music, or change and have a shower while the food looks after itself. For the recipes with the longest cooking time, you can even go out for a long walk or pop down to the gym while the oven does its work.

As food writers running a creative food business, with husbands who are equally busy, we find these dishes serve us really well. Using fresh and store-cupboard ingredients, these fully-tested, foolproof recipes provide us with a wonderful variety of freshly cooked meals. To make things even easier, there are plenty of serving suggestions and hints and tips to go with the recipes. So remember, when time is tight, you can always use your oven to cook healthy and delicious meals.

RECIPE GUIDELINES

We have used two symbols to help you choose the right type of recipe for the time you have available, because some of the recipes are quick from start to finish whereas others will bubble or simmer away while you are doing something else.

For recipes which require around 30 minutes or less in the oven, look for this symbol of a plate of food:

Alternatively, if you aren't in a hurry to eat and your meal can be left to cook in the oven for a longer time, choose one of the recipes with this symbol of a book and a mug:

Recipes without a symbol are mostly cooked in 1 hour or less and may require a little extra attention to detail, or an ingredient added part way through cooking, or perhaps the cooked dish needs cooling before serving.

For convenience, the ingredients are listed in the order in which they are used. Though they are given in imperial measurements as well as metric, you will find the metric easier to use.

All spoon measurements are level unless otherwise stated.

Most of the recipes can produce extra servings, simply by doubling the quantity of ingredients.

The recipes include basic store-cupboard ingredients, including the occasional stock cube and, our favourite, vegetable bouillon powder. Because it's granular, you can spoon out as little as you like. Our store cupboard always contains canned tomatoes, canned beans, and pastes that are quick and convenient – garlic, curry and chilli.

A few recipes contain fresh chillies. Do take care when preparing them and remember to wash your hands thoroughly afterwards. Or wear rubber gloves while handling them.

One or two recipes may contain raw or partly cooked eggs – please remember that it is advisable to avoid eating these if you are pregnant, elderly, very young or sick.

Salt is kept to a minimum. Instead, we prefer to source good quality ingredients that have bags of flavour. In the oven, these flavours are left to intermingle. Then all that may be needed is a simple last-minute addition or topping to add interest, texture, extra flavour or an instant burst of freshness.

The equipment is kept simple. You will need just the usual oven utensils – a roasting tin, baking sheets and ovenproof casserole dishes. A flameproof casserole for using on the hob is handy too, though not essential. Remember, cooking in one dish will save on washing up.

In some of the recipes you will notice that the ingredients are browned quickly in a pan or flameproof casserole on the hob before putting them in the oven. This is not essential, though it will improve the colour and flavour of the finished dish. If you can't spare the time, simply omit this step.

In the recipes the oven is preheated. If you use a fan oven, preheating may not be needed; check your instruction book.

Oven Temperature Conversion Chart
Ovens vary from model to model – use this chart as a guide only.

Electric °C	Fan °C	Gas Mark
100	100	¼
110	110	¼
130	115	½
140	125	1
150	135	2
160	145	3
180	165	4
190	175	5
200	185	6
220	205	7
230	215	8
250	235	9

1

START THE DAY

Going to the gym, or out for a walk? Are weekday business activities or weekend leisure pursuits taking up your time? That can mean that breakfast is rushed or neglected altogether. So here are some ideas to help you start the day right.

If you cook porridge long and slow overnight, you can forget about it until you need it. Other things to be made in advance include oat-and-yogurt bars, apple cake, and homemade granola in place of your usual cereal. There are also some recipes for larger numbers or mega-breakfasts. Whether you want the works (bacon, egg and all the trimmings) or muffins, filled croissants, sausage and egg slice or vegetarian breakfast pastries, it's here. While these are cooking, enjoy your fruit juice and find time to relax.

breakfast pizza

Oven Porridge

Simply leave the oats and water in the oven overnight. By the morning, the porridge will be thick and creamy and can be left until you have had that early morning walk or a lazy lie-in. Think of cooking a dish of mixed dried fruit at the same time (see below) – serve it with the porridge or save it for another meal.

Serves 4

1. Put 175g/6 oz whole rolled oats or porridge oats into an ovenproof dish and pour over 1.4 litres/2½ pints boiling water (from the kettle).

2. Cover securely and cook at 100°C, Fan 100°C, Gas ¼ for 8–12 hours.

3. Serve with your favourite additions – a little salt, sugar, milk, cream, and so on.

Warm Fruits

Dried fruits plump up beautifully in the low heat of the oven. No need for specific quantities here – cook as much as you like. Try a mixture of dried apricots, apples, prunes and sultanas (and add a little brown sugar or honey if you have a sweet tooth). Lovely served warm or cold.

Serves as many as you like

1. Put your chosen fruit mixture into an ovenproof casserole and add orange juice or apple juice to cover it by about 2cm/¾ inch.

2. Cover securely and cook at 100°C, Fan 100°C, Gas ¼ for 8–12 hours.

Granola

A breakfast treat made with a combination of oats, nuts and dried fruits. We've 'toasted' the mix and added an oil-and-honey glaze to give a more crisp-and-crunchy effect. Vary the recipe each time you make it, adding your favourite nuts and dried fruits. When cool, store in an airtight container and use within two weeks. Serve with milk, natural yogurt or fruit juice.

Serves 8–10

2 tbsp olive oil
4 tbsp clear honey
3 tbsp malt extract
150g/5½ oz jumbo oats
150g/5½ oz wheat flakes
150g/5½ oz rye flakes
60g/2¼ oz sunflower seeds
60g/2¼ oz pumpkin seeds
200g/7 oz sultanas

1. Preheat the oven to 140°C, Fan 125°C, Gas 1.

2. Heat the oil in a saucepan over a low heat and stir in the honey and malt extract. When hot and melted, remove from the heat and stir in the remaining ingredients except the sultanas.

3. Spread the mixture in a shallow layer on one or two baking sheets.

4. Put into the preheated oven and cook for 1 hour until the cereals and seeds are crisp and crunchy.

5. Leave to cool completely, and then stir in the sultanas. Store in an airtight container (see note above).

The Works

You could stand at the hob cooking one ingredient at a time, or you could try this easy routine for cooking sausage, bacon, egg and all the trimmings in the oven. Increase or reduce the quantities as necessary and don't worry about crowding it all into the oven. Either serve the eggs still in their dishes or run a knife round the edge and slide them out onto the plates with the rest of the breakfast.

Serves 6

6 large sausages, about 400–450g/14–16 oz total weight
Oil
415g can baked beans
12 back bacon rashers
6 medium tomatoes
6 thick slices of black pudding
6 large open-cup or flat mushrooms
6 medium eggs

1. Preheat the oven to 190°C, Fan 175°C, Gas 5.

2. Separate the sausages and arrange them on a large, lightly oiled baking sheet, leaving plenty of space between them. Tip the baked beans into an ovenproof dish and cover with foil. Put the sausages and beans into the hot oven and cook for 15 minutes.

3. Meanwhile, with scissors, trim the rind from the bacon. Cut the tomatoes in half.

4. Leaving the beans in the oven, turn the hot sausages over and push them close together. Now add the bacon to the hot baking sheet, overlapping the rashers so that all the fatty edges are facing upwards and only the meat on the last rasher is visible. Add the tomato halves, sitting some of them on the meaty part of the exposed bacon (to prevent it becoming dry) and the black pudding. Return to the hot oven and cook for a further 10 minutes.

5. Meanwhile, brush the mushrooms lightly with oil and put onto another baking sheet. Brush six small ovenproof dishes or ramekins with oil and break an egg into each.

6. Add the mushrooms and eggs to the hot oven (using two or even three shelves) and cook for the final 8–10 minutes until the eggs are just set. Serve immediately.

Baked Breakfast Eggs with Smoked Trout

Perfect for breakfast or brunch, serve them with sliced, toasted bagels.

Serves 4

50g/1¾ oz butter
140g/5 oz cooked smoked trout
1 tsp lemon juice
4 tbsp single cream
1 tbsp freshly chopped parsley
4 medium eggs
Freshly milled black pepper

1. Preheat the oven to 180°C, Fan 165°C, Gas 4. Thickly butter four individual ovenproof dishes about the size of small cereal bowls.

2. Skin and flake the trout, removing any bones, and put in a small bowl. Stir in the lemon juice, cream and parsley and divide between the dishes.

3. Make a small well in the centre of the fish mixture, break an egg in the dip and shake a little pepper on top.

4. Stand the dishes on a baking sheet, put into the hot oven and cook for 5–10 minutes until the eggs are just set and the fish is piping hot.

5. Serve immediately.

Breakfast Pastries

Perfect for vegetarians and meat-eaters alike. Crisp pastry cases filled with two cheeses, eggs, spinach and tomatoes. You will need six 10cm/4 inch individual tartlet tins, or use Yorkshire pudding tins instead. For speed we've used ready-rolled short-crust pastry. Pimento is a type of Spanish, sweet, red pepper; here we've used bottled or canned ones which are already skinned. Eat the pastries hot or cold.

Serves 6

375g packet ready-rolled shortcrust pastry
9 cherry tomatoes
Large handful of baby spinach leaves
200g/7 oz pimentos (see note above)
200g packet feta cheese
6 small eggs
Freshly milled black pepper
1 tbsp Parmesan cheese

1. Preheat the oven to 200°C, Fan 185°C, Gas 6.
2. Unroll the pastry, cut in half along the length, and then cut each half into three to make six squares. Drape one pastry square over a tartlet tin and with your thumbs press the pastry into the hollow. With a sharp knife, trim off any excess pastry. Repeat with the remaining squares.
3. With a fork, prick the base of each pastry case then put a scrunched piece of foil into each (this prevents the pastry from rising as it cooks). Stand the tins on a baking sheet.
4. Put into the hot oven and cook for 15 minutes. Remove from the oven and carefully remove the foil.
5. Slice the tomatoes in half, chop the spinach, chop the pimentos and crumble the feta cheese.
6. Divide the spinach and pimentos between the pastry cases and top with some of the feta. Push the mixture towards the edge of the pastry cases and break an egg into the centre of each. Top with the tomato halves, a little pepper and the Parmesan cheese.
7. Put into the hot oven and cook for 10–15 minutes until the egg is just set and the pastry is golden.

Mushroom and Tomato Tart with Crisp Bacon

This brunch dish is quick to prepare with a ready-made pastry case. If you like, sprinkle a little grated cheese over the top of the tart before cooking. Any left over is good served cold.

Serves 4

20cm/8 inch cooked plain pastry case
6 cherry tomatoes
4 chestnut mushrooms
2 medium eggs
1 generous tsp wholegrain mustard
150g/5½ oz soft cheese such as quark or ricotta
Freshly milled salt and black pepper
8 bacon rashers

1. Preheat the oven to 190°C, Fan 175°C, Gas 5.

2. Put the pastry case (still in its foil tray) on a baking sheet.

3. Halve the cherry tomatoes and quarter the mushrooms. Lightly beat the eggs, add the mustard and cheese and, with a whisk, beat well until smooth and thick. Season lightly with salt and pepper.

4. Scatter the tomatoes and mushrooms in the pastry case and spoon the egg mixture evenly over the top.

5. Put into the hot oven and cook for 10 minutes.

6. Meanwhile, lay the bacon on another baking sheet or roasting tin, with the rashers slightly overlapping and the fat edges up.

7. Put the bacon into the hot oven with the tart and continue cooking for a further 20 minutes until the egg mixture is set and golden brown and the bacon is cooked.

8. Serve the tart cut into wedges and topped with the crisp bacon.

Sausage, Egg and Bacon Slice

Delicious and filling for breakfast, but ideal to serve (hot or cold) for lunch or supper too. Serve it with warm crusty bread.

Serves 4–6

4 medium eggs
1 medium onion
4 smoked back-bacon rashers
150g/5½ oz chestnut mushrooms
250g/9 oz sausage meat
3 tbsp freshly chopped parsley
Freshly milled black pepper
375g packet ready-rolled shortcrust pastry
2 tbsp milk

1. Hard-boil the eggs for 10 minutes, drain and, when cold, peel off the shells and cut in half lengthways.
2. Finely chop the onion. With scissors, trim the rind from the bacon and chop the bacon finely. Clean, trim and finely chop the mushrooms.
3. Heat a small pan, add the bacon and cook for about 5 minutes, stirring occasionally, until golden brown and some of the fat has run out. With a slotted spoon, transfer the bacon to a large bowl and leave to cool. Put the onion in the hot pan, reduce the heat and cook for 5 minutes, stirring occasionally, until soft but not browned. Lift out of the pan and add to the bacon.
4. Preheat the oven to 200°C, Fan 185°C, Gas 6.
5. To the cooled bacon mixture, add the sausage meat, mushrooms, parsley and a little pepper. With a fork, mix thoroughly, breaking up the sausage meat.
6. Unroll the pastry onto a baking sheet. Spoon the bacon-and-sausage mixture down the length of the pastry, keeping it away from the edges. Lightly press the egg halves into the sausage mixture. Brush the edges of the pastry with milk and fold the two long sides over the filling, overlapping them and pressing until sealed. Carefully turn the roll over with the seam underneath. Brush the top with milk and, with a sharp knife, make a few diagonal slashes in the pastry.
7. Put in the hot oven and cook for 30–40 minutes until crisp, golden and cooked through.

Breakfast Pizza

Pizza fans will love this for brunch. In place of pizza bases, use your favourite flatbreads.

Serves 2

400g can chopped tomatoes
About 8 mushrooms, such as chestnut
4 frankfurters
4 bacon rashers
2 ready-made pizza bases, each measuring about
 20–22.5cm/8–9 in
2 eggs
Grated Cheddar or Edam cheese
Olive oil (optional)

1. Preheat the oven to 220°C, Fan 205°C, Gas 7.

2. Tip the tomatoes into a sieve and leave them to drain while you prepare the other ingredients.

3. Clean and trim the mushrooms and slice thickly. Cut the frankfurters in half lengthways. With scissors, trim the rind from the bacon and cut the bacon into wide strips.

4. Put the pizza bases onto one or two baking sheets. Spread the tomatoes on top and scatter the mushroom slices over. Lay four frankfurter halves in the centre of each pizza, in a square shape (this will form the frame to contain the egg). Arrange the bacon pieces round the edges. Break an egg into each frankfurter 'frame'. Sprinkle some grated cheese over the top of the pizzas and, if liked, drizzle with some olive oil.

5. Put into the hot oven and cook for about 10 minutes until the pizza edges are crisp and golden and the bacon and eggs are cooked. Serve immediately.

Hot Filled Croissants

Why not offer a choice of fillings so that your guests can choose their own?

Serves as many as you like

1. Preheat the oven to 200°C, Fan 185°C, Gas 6.

2. Split croissants and fill with the mixture of your choice –
    see the suggestions below.

3. Put the filled croissants onto a baking sheet.

4. Put into the hot oven and cook for a few minutes until crisp
    on the outside and warmed through.

Savoury Fillings:

Ham and Cheese
Into the split croissant, put a slice or two of ham (cooked or
cured) and a thin slice of cheese – Gruyère or Gouda are
particularly nice, though Cheddar-type cheeses are good too.

Cream Cheese, Tomatoes, Olives and Basil
Spoon a generous amount of cream cheese onto the bottom
half of the croissant and add some strips of sun-dried tomato,
sliced olives (green or black) and a few fresh basil leaves. Top
with the other half of the croissant.

Soft Cheese, Mustard and Ham
Spread one half thickly with soft cheese such as fromage frais,
quark or ricotta and the other half with wholegrain mustard. Add
a thick slice of ham and sandwich the halves together again.

Tuna Mayonnaise, Spring Onions and Capers
Flake some drained canned tuna and stir in enough mayonnaise
to bind it together. Add chopped spring onions, capers and
fresh herbs (try parsley, thyme, dill or fennel).

Blue Cheese, Walnuts and Celery
With a fork, mash the cheese (try Stilton, Roquefort or Dolce-
latte) lightly and stir in a few chopped walnuts and a little finely
chopped celery.

Roast Beef with Horseradish, Tomato and Spinach

Spread a little horseradish sauce over the cut surfaces of the croissant and add a thick slice of roast beef, some thin slices of tomato and a few spinach leaves.

Chicken, Tomato and Pesto

Spread green or red pesto on the split croissant and add tomato slices and plenty of cooked chicken.

Sweet Fillings:

Banana, Maple Syrup and Walnuts

Tuck thick slices of banana into the split croissant, drizzling them with maple syrup and adding a few chopped walnuts or pecans.

Cottage Cheese and Fruit

Fill the croissant with a generous spoonful of cottage cheese, some soft fruit (such as raspberries, blackberries, blueberries or sliced strawberries) and a sprinkling of brown sugar.

Strawberries and Cream

Warm the croissant in the oven first, and then fill with whipped cream or clotted cream, a small spoonful of strawberry jam and some sliced fresh strawberries.

Pear with Chocolate and Hazelnut Spread

Cover the cut surfaces of the croissant with chocolate and hazelnut spread, and then fill with slices of ripe pear.

Mascarpone, Fig and Honey

Fill the croissant with a generous amount of mascarpone or other creamy cheese, some slices of fresh fig and a drizzle of clear honey.

Blueberry and Orange Muffins

Muffins are so easy to make, it's success every time. You don't have to be a great cake-maker to get superb results. The ingredients are mixed only until they are just combined, rather than beating until light and fluffy as in a sponge cake. We've used blueberries, but for a change use whole fresh or dried blackcurrants, raspberries or redcurrants, or finely chopped apple, banana or peaches.

Makes 12

200g/7 oz wholemeal self-raising flour
60g/2¼ oz self-raising flour
1 tsp baking powder
2 medium eggs
50g/1¾ oz light brown sugar
4 tbsp olive oil
250ml/9 fl oz milk
2 tsp grated orange rind
60g/2¼ oz blueberries

1. Preheat the oven to 200°C, Fan 185°C, Gas 6.

2. Sift the two flours and baking powder into a large bowl, tipping any grain particles left in the sieve into the bowl. Break the eggs into the flour and add the sugar, oil, milk, orange rind and blueberries.

3. With a wooden spoon, lightly beat the ingredients together until they are just mixed (don't worry if the mixture is still a little lumpy – it's important not to over-mix). Spoon into the muffin cases.

4. Put into the hot oven and cook for 15–20 minutes until risen and firm to the touch. Turn out onto a cooling rack.

5. Serve warm or cool.

Oat and Yogurt Bars

Quite soft and almost cake like, these bars taste good at any time of the day. You could add a small handful of chocolate chips to the mixture in step 3.

Makes 16 squares

175g/6 oz whole rolled oats
75g/2¾ oz soft brown sugar
50g/1¾ oz plain wholemeal flour
2 tbsp sesame seeds
½ tsp baking powder
1 tsp ground mixed spice
50g/1¾ oz walnut or pecan pieces
50g/1¾ oz dried apricots
4 tbsp olive oil
150g carton natural yogurt
1 large egg
1 tsp vanilla extract

1. Lightly grease a 20cm/8 in square cake tin.

2. Preheat the oven to 180°C, Fan 165°C, Gas 4.

3. Put the oats into a large mixing bowl and stir in the sugar, flour, seeds, baking powder and mixed spice, mixing well.

4. Roughly chop the nuts and apricots and stir them into the oat mixture.

5. Whisk together the oil, yogurt, egg and vanilla. Stir the liquid into the dry ingredients, mixing well.

6. Tip into the prepared tin, spreading the mixture to the edges and levelling the surface.

7. Put into the hot oven and cook for about 25 minutes until golden brown and set.

8. Leave to cool in the tin until quite firm, then, using a sharp knife, mark and cut into squares. Carefully lift the pieces onto a wire rack and leave to cool completely.

Apple Cinnamon Cake

Serve this moist and delicious cake warm or cold with a cup of good, strong coffee. Make sure the butter is soft before you mix the cake in step 4.

Makes about 12 slices

250g/9 oz self-raising flour
1½ tsp ground cinnamon
175g/6 oz soft dark brown sugar
175g/6 oz soft butter or margarine
3 medium eggs
4 tbsp apple juice or milk
2 medium cooking apples, such as Bramley, total weight about 500g/1 lb 2 oz
Icing sugar for dusting

1. Grease a 20cm/8 in round cake tin (preferably one with a removable base) and line it with baking paper.

2. Preheat the oven to 180°C, Fan 165°C, Gas 4.

3. Sift the flour and cinnamon into a large mixing bowl and add the sugar and butter or margarine. Lightly beat the eggs with the apple juice or milk. Peel the apples, quarter and remove the cores and chop into small pieces.

4. Add the egg mixture to the flour mixture and beat well until smooth and light (use a wooden spoon or an electric mixer). Stir in the apples.

5. Spoon the mixture into the prepared tin and gently level the top.

6. Put into the hot oven and cook for about 1 hour 10 minutes or until the cake is golden brown, firm to the touch and a thin skewer inserted in the centre comes out clean with no uncooked cake mixture stuck to it.

7. Leave the cake in the tin for 15–20 minutes before carefully turning it out and leaving on a wire rack to cool.

8. Serve in wedges with some icing sugar sifted over the top.

2

STRICTLY VEGETABLES

For vegetables read variety. Pies, tarts, frittata, gratins, pot roast or casseroles, whatever you want you'll find it here. These strictly-vegetable dishes are ideal for vegetarians and non-vegetarians alike. Try Tomato, Feta and Mint Tart (on page 35), or Slow-Cooked Roots (on page 26), or maybe Vegetable Medley with Cheese and Chive Dumplings (on page 30).

Some dishes contain cheese, and vegetarians will want to select the vegetarian versions of those particular cheeses. Non-vegetarians can always add a little meat or fish to any of these recipes.

Are you feeding a crowd? There's no problem – all the recipes are suitable for doubling up and most need only the addition of salad or bread.

Extra vegetable recipes appear in other sections too.

hot beans and vegetables

Slow-Cooked Roots

Choose your own favourite vegetable selection – they don't need to be exclusively root vegetables. Try replacing the turnips with courgettes, a small aubergine or red peppers. Eat as a supper dish, or as an accompaniment to roasts.

Serves 6

450g/1 lb potatoes
4 medium carrots
3 medium parsnips
2 small turnips
2 large onions
2 large garlic cloves
Small bunch of fresh parsley
300ml/½ pint chicken or vegetable stock
300ml/½ pint milk
2 tbsp olive oil
Freshly milled salt and black pepper
50g/1¾ oz butter

1. Peel and thinly slice the potatoes, carrots, parsnips, turnips and onions. Crush the garlic and finely chop the parsley.

2. Pour the stock, milk and oil into a large jug and stir in the garlic, parsley and plenty of seasoning.

3. Use a little of the butter to grease a large ovenproof casserole. Fill with layers of vegetables adding some of the liquid to each layer.

4. Dot the remaining butter on top.

5. Cover, put in the oven and cook at 180°C, Fan 165°C, Gas 4 for 1–1¼ hours or until the vegetables are soft.

Baked Sweet Potato and Tomato

Good served as a main dish (perhaps with extra cheese on top) or as an accompaniment to roast chicken. We like to leave the skins on the sweet potatoes. Squash would make a good alternative to sweet potato (but remove its skin first). Instead of Parmesan, choose your favourite cheese (grated) for sprinkling on top. A few capers or sliced black olives could be tucked under the vegetables too.

Serves 4–6

1 large onion
2 tbsp olive oil
4 large tomatoes
2 large sweet potatoes
1–2 tbsp chopped fresh oregano or marjoram (optional)
Freshly milled salt and black pepper
150ml/¼ pint vegetable stock
2–3 tbsp grated Parmesan cheese

1. Preheat the oven to 180°C, Fan 165°C, Gas 4.

2. Thinly slice the onion and toss the slices in 1 tbsp oil. Slice the tomatoes. Scrub the sweet potatoes and slice them thinly.

3. Brush a shallow ovenproof dish with the remaining oil. Arrange the tomatoes and sweet potatoes in the dish in rows, sprinkling the oregano or marjoram between the layers. Scatter the oiled onion over the top and season lightly with salt and pepper. Pour the stock over.

4. Cover the dish securely with foil, put into the hot oven and cook for about 1¼-1½ hours until the vegetables are soft.

5. Remove the foil, top with the cheese and cook for 15–30 minutes until the top is golden brown.

Baked Onion and Vegetable Stacks

Onions, potatoes and tomatoes form these stacks. As they cook, their flavours merge and mingle. Serve for a light supper, or with sausages for a main meal.

Serves 4

4 large onions
1 large potato
2 beefsteak tomatoes
Small piece of butter
300ml/½ pint vegetable or chicken stock
2 tbsp freshly chopped parsley
1 tbsp olive oil

1. Preheat the oven to 190°C, Fan 175°C, Gas 5.

2. Cut the onions in half across the middle. Peel the potato and cut into 4 thick slices. Cut the tomatoes in half.

3. Butter the inside of a square or oblong ovenproof dish. Arrange the potato slices in a single layer in the base of the dish (they should be a snug fit). Stand the tomatoes on top and then the onion halves. Don't worry if the stacks seem high, the tomatoes will cook down during cooking. Pour the stock over, then sprinkle with the parsley and drizzle with the oil.

4. Cover, put in the hot oven and cook for 1–1½ hours until the onion is tender.

Braised Fennel, Celeriac and Celery with Walnut Topping

Of these three vegetables, fennel and celery are probably the more familiar, but celeriac has a lovely flavour too. This knobbly root tastes like a cross between celery and parsley. It can be eaten raw or cooked but does discolour quickly – if you prepare it in advance put it in cold water with a little lemon juice.

Serves 4–6

4 large fennel bulbs
1 small celeriac
2 celery heads
6 shallots
1 lemon
300ml/½ pint vegetable stock
Freshly milled black pepper
6 tbsp plain flour
60g/2¼ oz butter
60g/2¼ oz walnut pieces
2 tbsp fresh oregano leaves or 2 tsp dried oregano

1. Trim the fennel bulbs and cut each into eight wedges. Peel the celeriac and cut into bite-size pieces. Trim the celery and cut into finger lengths. Peel and halve the shallots. Halve the lemon and squeeze out the juice.

2. Put the vegetables in an ovenproof casserole and stir in the lemon juice, stock and pepper.

3. For the topping, put the flour and butter in a medium bowl. Using your fingertips or a fork, rub the butter into the flour until the mixture resembles breadcrumbs. Stir in the walnuts and oregano leaves. Scatter the crumb mixture over the vegetables and press down gently.

4. Cover, put into the oven and cook at 180°C, Fan 165°C, Gas 4 for about 1 hour or until the vegetables are tender, removing the lid for the final 10 minutes to brown the top.

Vegetable Medley with Cheese and Chive Dumplings

Don't be put off by the long list of ingredients – this is really easy. Everything goes into the pot, which is then put in the oven and left to cook – all you have to do is add the dumplings about 30 minutes before you want to eat. Vary the vegetables according to what's available. It's best to heat the stock before adding it to the vegetables – for ease, dissolve stock cubes or vegetable bouillon powder with boiling water from the kettle. Though the tahini (or sesame paste) is optional, it does help to thicken and add a richness to the sauce.

Serves 4–6

1 large onion
2 large celery stalks
3 medium carrots
2 medium parsnips
2 medium potatoes
1 small swede
1 medium fennel bulb
4 sun-dried tomatoes
1 garlic clove
400g can red kidney beans
600ml/1 pint vegetable stock, preferably hot
1 tbsp tomato purée
1 tbsp tahini (sesame paste)
1 generous tsp fennel seeds
1 generous tbsp wholegrain mustard

Dumplings:
175g/6 oz self-raising flour
Freshly milled salt and black pepper
40g/1½ oz butter
50g/1¾ oz Parmesan cheese
2 tbsp chopped chives or spring onion tops (green parts only)
1 medium egg
2–3 tbsp milk

1. Preheat the oven to 180°C, Fan 165°C, Gas 4.

2. Roughly chop the onion. Thickly slice the celery, carrots and parsnips. Cut the potatoes and swede into small cubes and thinly slice the fennel. Cut the tomatoes into small pieces and finely chop the garlic. Tip everything into a large ovenproof casserole and stir in the red beans (including their liquid).

3. Whisk or stir together the hot stock, tomato purée, tahini and fennel seeds. Pour the mixture over the vegetables and stir well.

4. Cover, put into the hot oven and cook for 2–2¼ hours until the vegetables are just tender.

5. About 10 minutes before the end of cooking, make the dumplings. Sift the flour into a mixing bowl and season lightly with salt and pepper. Cut the butter into small pieces and add to the flour. With your fingertips, rub the butter into the flour until the mixture resembles fine breadcrumbs. Stir in the Parmesan cheese and chives or spring onion tops. Break the egg into the mixture and add the milk. Using a flat-end knife and a cutting action, mix the egg and milk into the flour until you are able to gather the mixture into a ball of soft dough. Divide it into 12 small pieces or balls.

6. Stir the mustard gently into the vegetables. Arrange the dumplings on top, cover and cook for 20 minutes or until the dumplings have risen.

7. Remove the lid and increase the heat to 200°C, Fan 185°C, Gas 6. Return the casserole to the oven and cook for a further 10 minutes or until the dumplings are crisp and golden brown on top and the vegetables are soft.

Hot Beans and Vegetables with Garlic Toasts

Topped with slices of crisp garlic bread, this is a filling and warming dish. Meat-eaters could replace half the beans with skinless, boneless chopped chicken or turkey. Serve with a large mixed salad.

Serves 6–8

1 medium onion
2 garlic cloves
1 red chilli (see page 8)
Thumb-length piece of root ginger
Small bunch of parsley
2 medium carrots
400g can flageolet beans
400g can cannellini beans
1 tbsp vegetable bouillon powder
½ tsp cayenne pepper
4 tbsp mango chutney
Freshly milled salt and black pepper
1 tbsp olive oil
6–8 slices French bread stick
2 tbsp grated Parmesan cheese

1. Preheat the oven to 190°C, Fan 175°C, Gas 5.
2. Roughly chop the onion and crush the garlic. Cut the chilli in half, remove and discard the seeds and stalk and slice thinly. Grate the ginger and chop the parsley. Thinly slice the carrots. Drain the beans.
3. Put the onion and half the garlic into a medium ovenproof dish. Add the carrots, drained beans, chilli, ginger and parsley. Stir in the bouillon, cayenne, mango chutney and some seasoning.
4. Cover, put into the hot oven and cook for 1 hour.
5. Meanwhile, mix the oil with the remaining garlic and brush over the bread slices. Sprinkle the cheese over.
6. Remove the cover and increase the oven heat to 200°C, Fan 185°C, Gas 6. Arrange the bread slices on top of the bean mixture and continue cooking, uncovered, for a further 15 minutes until the bread slices are crisp and golden.

Aubergines and Courgettes with Mixed Nuts

We've made a vegetarian version of the classic Greek dish moussaka. It's so tasty you won't miss the meat. It needs only a green salad to complete the meal.

Serves 4

2 medium aubergines
2 large courgettes
1 large onion
2 garlic cloves
2 tbsp olive oil
200g/7 oz mixed unsalted nuts, such as peanuts, walnuts, cashews or blanched almonds
Small bunch of fresh parsley
85g/3 oz Cheddar cheese
400ml/14 fl oz milk
3 medium eggs
¼ tsp grated nutmeg
Freshly milled salt and black pepper

1. Preheat the oven to 200°C, Fan 185°C, Gas 6.

2. Trim and slice the aubergines, courgettes and onion. Finely chop the garlic.

3. Arrange the aubergines, courgettes and onion in a single layer on one or two baking sheets. Brush both sides of the vegetables very lightly with oil. Put in the hot oven and cook for 15 minutes until lightly browned.

4. Reduce the oven temperature to 180°C, Fan 165°C, Gas 4.

5. Roughly chop the nuts and parsley. Grate the cheese. Pour the milk into a large jug and beat in the eggs and nutmeg, Stir in half the cheese and some seasoning.

6. Put half the vegetables into a medium ovenproof dish, scatter over the garlic, nuts and parsley, then add the remaining vegetables. Use tongs if the vegetables are still warm.

7. Pour the egg mixture over and scatter with the remaining cheese.

8. Put into the hot oven and cook uncovered for about 20 minutes until the top has set and lightly browned.

Mediterranean Omelette

Similar to Spain's tortilla and Italy's frittata, this large flat vegetable omelette can be served hot with a crisp salad or cold tucked between slices of bread. Try adding other ingredients too, like chilli, olives, bacon or slices of spicy sausage.

Serves 6–8

1 large red or white onion
1 large potato
2 medium carrots
2 medium courgettes
1 red pepper
1–2 garlic cloves
3 tbsp olive oil
10 medium eggs
Freshly milled salt and pepper
Small handful of mint leaves
Small handful of parsley
4–5 tbsp freshly grated Parmesan cheese

1. Preheat the oven to 220°C, Fan 205°C, Gas 7.

2. Finely chop the onion. Cut the potato, carrots and courgettes into small cubes. Halve the pepper, remove and discard the seeds and stalk, and cut into small pieces. Finely chop the garlic cloves. Toss all the vegetables with the olive oil and garlic until well coated (do this in a food/freezer bag or large bowl).

3. Spread the oiled vegetables in a shallow, non-stick baking tray or swiss roll tin, measuring about 27 x 36cm/11 x 13 inches. Put into the hot oven and cook for about 30 minutes, stirring once or twice, until golden brown and just soft.

4. Meanwhile, beat the eggs, seasoning with salt and pepper. Finely chop the mint and parsley and stir them into the eggs.

5. Pour the eggs over the hot vegetables, tilting the pan to spread the mixture evenly. Sprinkle the Parmesan over the top.

6. Continue cooking for a further 7–10 minutes until the egg is puffed up, set and golden brown.

7. Cut into portions and serve.

Tomato, Feta and Mint Tart

Serve warm with a leafy salad, black olives and some Italian ciabatta bread. For ease, use a ready-made pastry case.

Serves 4

Handful of fresh mint leaves
1 large tomato
200g packet feta cheese
2 medium eggs
150ml/¼ pint double cream
Freshly milled black pepper
20cm/8 inch cooked pastry case

1. Preheat the oven to 190°C, Fan 175°C, Gas 5.

2. Roughly chop the mint leaves. Thinly slice the tomato. Crumble the feta cheese or cut it into small cubes. Break the eggs into a bowl, add the cream and a little black pepper and beat well.

3. Put the pastry case (still in its foil tray) on a baking sheet. Spread the chopped mint in the base and top with the tomato and then the cheese. Pour the egg mixture over the top.

4. Put into the hot oven and cook for about 25 minutes or until golden brown and set.

Mediterranean Filo

A dish of two parts, firstly the filling which is a meal in itself, and secondly the completed filo pastry dish. Peppers, tomatoes, courgettes and aubergines are cooked until soft and collapsed. We've used the oven but it could be cooked on the hob for 30–40 minutes instead. The mouth-watering filling is encased in tissue-thin layers of filo pastry.

Serves 6–8

2 large onions
2 large garlic cloves
2 red peppers
3 medium courgettes
2 small aubergines
Large bunch of coriander
400g can tomatoes
2 tbsp tomato purée
2 tbsp dried mixed herbs
2 tbsp olive oil
300ml/½ pint chicken or vegetable stock
Freshly milled black pepper
100g/3½ oz butter
10 sheets of filo pastry, thawed if frozen

To make the filling:
1.   Preheat the oven to 180°C, Fan 165°C, Gas 4.

2.   Chop the onions and finely chop or crush the garlic. Halve the peppers, remove and discard the seeds and stalk, and cut into small pieces. Trim and chop the courgettes and aubergines. Finely chop the coriander.

3.   Put the vegetables, garlic and coriander into a large ovenproof dish. Stir in the tomatoes, tomato purée, mixed herbs, oil, stock and some black pepper.

4.   Cover, put in the hot oven and cook for 1–1¼ hours, until the vegetables are very soft and collapsed. Remove from the oven, ladle into a large bowl and leave to cool completely.

To make the pie:

1. Preheat the oven to 190°C, Fan 175°C, Gas 5.

2. Melt the butter (on the hob or in the microwave) and cool. Unroll the filo pastry, keeping it covered with clear film until needed.

3. Brush a small roasting tin or shallow ovenproof dish with a little butter and lay a pastry sheet in the base (it's fine if it comes up the sides of the dish). Repeat with four more pastry sheets

4. Spoon in the cold vegetable mixture, spreading it to cover the pastry.

5. Lay a pastry sheet over the filling and brush with a little butter. Repeat this process, using up the remaining pastry.

6. Put into the oven and cook for 40 minutes until the pastry is crisp and golden.

Goats' Cheese, Artichoke and Mushroom Tart

Trimming the pastry before cooking helps the edges to puff up evenly. Instead of spreading the pastry with pesto, try mustard (French or wholegrain) or black olive paste (tapenade). Depending on the type of goats' cheese, either slice it thickly or scoop small spoonfuls over the tart. Serve it with a salad of crisp leaves.

Serves 4

280g jar artichoke hearts in oil
250g/9 oz cherry tomatoes
150g/5½ oz mushrooms, such as chestnut
375g packet of ready-rolled puff pastry
4 tbsp pesto
200g/7 oz goats' cheese (see note above)
Freshly milled salt and black pepper

1. Preheat the oven to 200°C, Fan 185°C, Gas 6.

2. Drain the artichokes, reserving the oil, cut them into quarters and tip into a mixing bowl. Halve the tomatoes and mushrooms (or quarter them if large), add to the bowl and toss gently until well mixed.

3. Unroll the pastry onto a baking sheet and, with a sharp knife, trim off no more than 5mm/¼ inch from all sides.

4. Spread the pesto over the pastry, leaving a 2.5cm/1 inch strip clear along the edges. Spread the artichoke mixture over the pesto, again leaving the edges free. Arrange the cheese (see note above) on the vegetables and season lightly with salt and pepper. Finally, drizzle a little of the reserved artichoke oil over the cheese.

5. Put into the hot oven and cook for 25–30 minutes until the pastry is puffed and golden and the cheese is soft.

3

ALL SPICED UP

Spiced dishes cooked in the oven have one great advantage – the cooking doesn't have to stop at a precise time. If you get distracted and leave the dish in the oven slightly longer than planned, it won't burn. Instead, its flavours will just go on intensifying.

We use familiar spices such as curry powder (or paste), five-spice, cumin, coriander, and chilli for heat, and all the meals are quick to prepare. There are Indian-style curries, like dhal, biryani and dhansak, and lighter-spiced recipes, such as the seafood mix with Thai flavourings.

You can easily multiply the quantities to serve more people. Anything left over can be reheated the next day. As with the longer cooking, reheating increases the depth of flavours.

texas chilli

Spiced Beans, Cashews and Spinach

Plain basmati rice and mango chutney go well with this vegetable and nut dish.

Serves 4

1 large onion
1 large carrot
Small piece of fresh root ginger
2 garlic cloves
2 green chillies (see page 8)
400g can red kidney beans
1 tbsp oil
1 tsp ground cumin
1 tsp ground coriander
½ tsp turmeric
50g/1¾ oz ground almonds
75g/2¾ oz unsalted cashew nuts
2 large handfuls (about 150g/5½ oz) baby spinach leaves

1. Chop the onion and carrot. Grate the root ginger and crush the garlic. Finely chop the chillies. Drain the kidney beans.

2. Preheat the oven to 150°C, Fan 135°C, Gas 2.

3. Heat the oil in a flameproof casserole, add the onion and carrot and cook for about 5 minutes, stirring occasionally, until slightly softened but not browned.

4. Add the cumin, coriander, turmeric, root ginger, chillies and garlic and cook, stirring, for 1–2 minutes.

5. Stir in the beans, almonds, cashew nuts and 300ml/½ pint water and bring just to the boil.

6. Cover, put into the hot oven and cook for 1–1½ hours.

7. Just before serving, stir the spinach into the casserole, cover and return it to the oven for 5–10 minutes until wilted.

Green Lentil Dhal

A tasty mix of lentils and spices. There's a long list of pulses which can be substituted for the green lentils: the more usual red lentils, or chana (split yellow peas), or moong (green skin lentil), or urid (black skin, white lentil), or chickpeas, borlotti beans or red kidney beans. For a smoother version the dhal can be puréed. Serve as a perfect accompaniment to curried meat, fish, bean dishes and rice (such as oven-cooked rice on page 105).

Serves 4–6

2 medium onions
2 garlic cloves
2 tbsp olive oil
300g/10½ oz green lentils
400g can tomatoes
450ml/¾ pint chicken or vegetable stock
1 tbsp dried mixed herbs
Freshly milled salt and pepper

1. Chop the onions and finely chop or crush the garlic.

2. Heat a large flameproof casserole, add the oil and onions and cook over a medium heat for about 5 minutes, stirring occasionally, until lightly browned. Stir in the lentils, tomatoes, garlic, stock, herbs and seasoning. Bring just to the boil.

3. Cover, put into the oven and cook at 180°C, Fan 165°C, Gas 4 for 45–60 minutes or until the lentils are tender and most of the liquid has been absorbed. Add a little more stock if the mixture becomes too dry.

Curried Lentils, Carrots and Parsnips

A warming dhansak-style dish made with lentils. Try this vegetarian version made with filling root vegetables. The spices turn ordinary ingredients into something special. Serve as a main course or as an accompaniment to roasted or grilled meat/fish steaks.

Serves 6

2 medium onions
2 large carrots
2 medium parsnips
2 garlic cloves
Small piece of fresh root ginger
250g/9 oz red lentils
2 tbsp oil
2 tbsp medium curry paste
600ml/1 pint chicken or vegetable stock
1 tbsp garam masala
A large handful of spinach leaves
Freshly milled salt and black pepper

1. Thinly slice the onions and roughly chop the carrots and parsnips. Chop the garlic and grate the ginger. Wash the lentils in a bowl of cold water, removing any pieces that float to the top.

2. Preheat the oven to 180°C, Fan 165°C, Gas 4.

3. Heat the oil in a large flameproof casserole, add the onions, garlic, carrots and parsnips and cook over a medium heat for about 5 minutes, stirring occasionally, until they begin to brown.

4. Stir in the lentils, ginger, curry paste and stock. Stirring, bring just to the boil.

5. Cover, put into the hot oven and cook for 50 minutes, stirring once or twice, until cooked and soft.

6. Remove from the oven, uncover, stir in the garam masala and spinach leaves and season if necessary. Cover and return to the oven for 5 minutes until the spinach leaves have wilted.

Spiced Aubergines and Chickpeas with Almonds and Crème Fraîche

Simple ingredients can be transformed by the use of just one or two spices. Here we've used aromatic coriander seeds with their flavour of lemon, sage and caraway. Sometimes you can find tiny aubergines which look attractive too – use twelve in place of the two large ones in this recipe. Serve with lots of naan bread to mop up the delicious sauce.

Serves 4–6

2 large aubergines
1 large onion
2 garlic cloves
400g can chickpeas
2 tbsp oil
1 tbsp coriander seeds
2 tbsp medium curry powder
400g can tomatoes
150ml/¼ pint coconut milk
600ml/1 pint chicken or vegetable stock
2 tbsp ground almonds
2 tbsp freshly chopped coriander leaves
150ml/¼ pint crème fraîche
Freshly milled salt and black pepper

1. Preheat the oven to 180°C, Fan 165°C, Gas 4.

2. Trim the stalks from the aubergines and chop roughly. Thinly slice the onion and chop or crush the garlic. Drain the chickpeas.

3. Heat the oil in a flameproof casserole, add the coriander seeds and cook over a high heat for a second or two until they begin to pop. Reduce the heat and stir in the curry powder, tomatoes, coconut milk and stock. Bring just to the boil and stir in the aubergines, onion and garlic.

4. Cover, put in the hot oven and cook for 30 minutes.

5. Add the chickpeas, ground almonds and half the fresh coriander and mix thoroughly. Cover and cook for a further 15 minutes.

6. Stir in the crème fraîche and the remaining coriander, seasoning if necessary. Serve immediately.

Spiced Fish Pie

Crispy, golden cubes of bread create a quick topping, making a change from mashed potatoes or pastry. Choose your fish according to availability – pollack, cod, haddock, salmon. Think of adding some shelled prawns too. Serve the pie with a salad of dressed leaves.

Serves 4

675g/1½ lb skinless fish or steaks (see note above)
Large handful of watercress or rocket leaves
3 thick bread slices
100g/3½ oz mature Cheddar-style cheese
200g carton crème fraîche
1 tbsp curry paste
100g/3½ oz frozen peas
Freshly milled salt and pepper
25g/1 oz butter

1. Preheat the oven to 190°C, Fan 175°C, Gas 5.

2. Cut the fish into chunks and roughly chop the watercress or rocket. Cut the crusts off the bread and cut into cubes. Grate the cheese.

3. Tip the crème fraîche into a mixing bowl and stir in the curry paste. Add the fish, peas, watercress or rocket, and seasoning and mix well. Tip the mixture into a shallow ovenproof dish, measuring about 25 x 18cm/10 x 7 inches.

4. Melt the butter (on the hob or in the microwave). Toss the bread cubes in the melted butter and spoon them over the fish mixture in the dish. Scatter the cheese over the top.

5. Put the dish into the hot oven and cook for about 45 minutes until the bread is crisp and the fish is cooked through.

Seafood Thai Curry

Thai curries are light and fragrant with lemon grass as an important flavouring. Lemon grass looks a little like a spring onion and gives a sour-lemon flavour and fragrance. We've used green curry paste which is readily available from supermarkets; the red variety would be equally good in this dish. If you use frozen shellfish there is no need to thaw it first. Serve with rice and flat-bread.

Serves 4–6

1 red onion
2 garlic cloves
Finger-length piece of lemon grass
500g/1 lb 2 oz cooked, shelled seafood (choose a mix of prawns, mussels, cockles, sliced squid and salmon fillet)
1 tbsp olive oil
1 tbsp lime juice
1 tbsp green Thai curry paste
300ml/½ pint chicken or vegetable stock
150ml/¼ pint coconut milk
Small bunch of fresh coriander
Freshly milled black pepper

1. Preheat the oven to 190°C, Fan 175°C, Gas 5.

2. Finely chop the onion and crush the garlic. Slit the piece of lemon grass along its length. If necessary, cut the fish into bite-size pieces.

3. Put all the ingredients except the coriander and black pepper into an ovenproof casserole.

4. Cover, put in the hot oven and cook for 40 minutes.

5. Meanwhile, roughly chop the coriander.

6. Remove and discard the piece of lemon grass, stir in the coriander and season with pepper to taste.

7. Serve immediately.

Sausages and Peppers in Batter

Take away the peppers and the spices and you have toad in the hole. Try serving it with mango chutney and a salad with watercress and baby spinach leaves.

Serves 4

1 medium onion
2 red or yellow peppers
8 large meaty sausages
2 tbsp oil
125g/4½ oz plain flour
Pinch of salt
1 tsp ground coriander
½ tsp ground cumin
Pinch of chilli powder
150ml/¼ pint milk
1 medium egg

1. Preheat the oven to 220°C, Fan 205°C, Gas 7.

2. Thinly slice the onion. Halve the peppers, remove and discard their seeds and stalks, and cut into wide strips.

3. Arrange the sausages and peppers in a roasting tin, scatter the onion over and drizzle with the oil.

4. Put the tin into the hot oven and cook for 10–15 minutes until the fat is very hot and the sausages are beginning to brown.

5. Meanwhile, sift the flour, salt and spices into a bowl. Mix the milk with 150ml/¼ pint water. Break the egg into the flour and gradually mix in the milk mixture, beating well to make a smooth batter.

6. Lift the roasting tin out of the oven, quickly pour in the batter and return it to the hot oven.

7. Continue cooking for 40–45 minutes or until the batter is puffed up and golden brown.

8. Serve immediately.

Beef with Red Pepper and Spiced Rice

A biryani-style dish of fragrant rice, peppers and beef. Basmati is the best type of long-grain rice and literally means 'queen of fragrance', with a nut-like flavour. For a complete meal, serve with just natural yogurt and naan bread.

Serves 4

2 red peppers
1 large onion
2 large garlic cloves
350g/12 oz lean beef steak
2 tbsp olive oil
1 tsp mild curry powder
½ tsp ground cinnamon
350g/12 oz basmati rice
450ml/¾ pint chicken or vegetable stock
Freshly milled salt and black pepper
1 tbsp freshly chopped parsley
50g/1¾ oz toasted, flaked almonds
50g/1¾ oz sultanas

1. Preheat the oven to 190°C, Fan 175°C, Gas 5.

2. Cut the peppers in half, remove and discard the seeds and stalks, and chop roughly. Thinly slice the onion and crush the garlic. Trim any fat from the beef and slice thinly.

3. Heat a large flameproof casserole on the hob, add the oil and beef and cook quickly until lightly browned. Lift out of the pan with a slotted spoon.

4. Reduce the heat under the pan, add the peppers, onion and garlic and cook gently for a few minutes, stirring occasionally, until beginning to brown. Return the beef to the pan, stir in the curry powder, cinnamon, rice, stock and seasoning. Bring just to the boil.

5. Cover, put in the hot oven and cook for 45–55 minutes or until the rice is tender and has absorbed the liquid.

6. Before serving stir in the parsley, almonds and sultanas.

Texas Chilli

Make it as hot and spicy or as mild as you like by adjusting the quantity of chilli powder. Serve with crusty bread, with oven rice (see page 105) or jacket potatoes (see page 66).

Serves 4–6

2 large onions
3 garlic cloves
2 red or yellow peppers
1kg/2¼ lb braising steak
2 tbsp oil
2 tsp ground cumin
2 tsp chilli powder
2 tsp dried oregano
Two 400g cans chopped tomatoes
Freshly milled salt and pepper

1. Preheat the oven to 160°C, Fan 145°C, Gas 3.

2. Thinly slice the onions and crush or finely chop the garlic. Halve the peppers, remove and discard the seeds and stalks, and chop roughly. Cut the steak into chunks.

3. Heat the oil in a large flameproof casserole, add the steak and brown quickly on all sides. Lift out with a slotted spoon.

4. Add the onions, garlic and peppers to the casserole and cook over a medium heat for 5–10 minutes, stirring occasionally, until softened and beginning to brown. Stir in the cumin, chilli and oregano.

5. Return the steak and any juices to the pan and stir in the tomatoes and a little seasoning. Heat until the liquid just comes to the boil.

6. Cover and put into the hot oven for 1½–2 hours until the steak is tender.

Lamb Flavoured with Fenugreek

Fenugreek or 'methi' is used as a hard or ground spice, or as dried leaves. Readily available from supermarkets, we've used the seeds in this dish. They are pleasantly bitter, slightly sweet and can be used whole or ground. Try making this dish with other meats or poultry too. Serve with rice (page 105), dhal (page 41) and mango chutney.

Serves 4

2 medium onions
1 garlic clove
6 tomatoes
Small bunch of fresh coriander
3 medium carrots
500g/1 lb 2 oz lean boneless lamb
1 tbsp oil
2 tsp fenugreek seeds
1 tsp ground cumin
400ml/14 fl oz lamb or vegetable stock
Freshly milled salt and pepper

1. Thinly slice the onions and crush the garlic. Quarter the tomatoes and finely chop the coriander. Slice the carrots. Trim excess fat from the lamb and cut into bite-size pieces.

2. Preheat the oven to 180°C, Fan 165°C, Gas 4.

3. Heat the oil in a flameproof casserole, add the onions and lamb and cook over a medium heat for a few minutes until lightly browned on all sides.

4. Stir in the garlic, tomatoes, carrots, fenugreek, cumin, stock and half the coriander. Bring just to the boil.

5. Cover, put into the hot oven and cook for 1–1¼ hours, stirring once, until the meat is tender.

6. Remove the cover, stir in the remaining coriander and season if necessary.

Spiced Duck with Apples, Roast Potatoes and Cabbage

A complete meal for four in one roasting tin.

Serves 4

12–16 small potatoes
1 tbsp oil
Freshly milled salt and pepper
½ small cabbage
2 crisp eating apples, preferably with red skins
2 tsp five-spice powder
4 duck legs
300ml/½ pint chicken or vegetable stock

1. Preheat the oven to 180°C, Fan 165°C, Gas 4.

2. Peel or scrape the potatoes, leaving them whole. In a bowl or food (freezer) bag, toss them in the oil until coated, adding a little seasoning.

3. Remove the stalk from the cabbage and cut into four wedges. Quarter the apples, remove the cores and cut each quarter into two wedges. Sprinkle the five-spice powder evenly over the duck legs.

4. In a medium roasting tin, arrange the cabbage wedges close together at the centre. Scatter the apple on and around the cabbage and sit the duck legs on top, skin side up. Arrange the oiled potatoes around the edges and pour the stock into the tin.

5. Put into the hot oven and cook for 1¾-2 hours until the duck is very tender and the cabbage is cooked through, the apples are soft and the potatoes are crisp and golden.

6. Serve immediately.

4

SMART DINING FOR ONE & TWO

A delicious meal that is also fun to prepare. This is just what you want when dining alone or there are just the two of you. All of these recipes have you in mind.

Firstly, there are no irritating, fractional ingredients, no half a teaspoon, no quarter of an egg. Secondly, these are not dishes which require you to stand and stir. They all naturally need long slow cooking. So don't think they will be too much effort – the preparation is really easy and the results will be great.

Many of the dishes can be doubled up, so you can make twice the quantity, save half, refrigerate the rest and then reheat (in the oven of course) on the following day.

trout in a foil parcel

Creamy Eggs with Parma Ham

Cooked in individual ovenproof dishes, rich creamy eggs are complemented by the addition of Parma ham, pine nuts and Cheddar cheese. Serve with garlic bread and a green salad.

Serves 2

1 shallot
Small handful of pine nuts
6 slices of Parma ham
100g/3½ oz mature Cheddar cheese
4 tbsp milk
4 tbsp double cream
4 medium eggs
2 tbsp chopped parsley
Freshly milled black pepper
Small piece of butter

1. Preheat the oven to 180°C, Fan 165°C, Gas 4.

2. Finely chop or grate the shallot and roughly chop the pine nuts. With scissors, cut the Parma ham in wide strips. Coarsely grate the cheese.

3. Pour the milk and cream into a jug, and then break in the eggs. Beat with a fork and mix in the parsley and pepper.

4. Use the butter to grease the insides of two individual ovenproof dishes and stand them on a baking sheet.

5. Divide the shallot, pine nuts and ham between the dishes. Pour half of the egg mixture into each dish and stir with a fork. Scatter the cheese over the top.

6. Put into the hot oven and cook for 25–30 minutes until the egg mixture is golden and just firm.

Potato and Cheese Layer

A simple, filling meal that is just delicious served with a crisp salad.

Serves 2

50g/1¾ oz butter, plus extra for greasing
500g/1 lb 2 oz potatoes
1 medium onion
1 garlic clove (optional)
4 fresh sage leaves
100g/3½ oz cheese, such as Cheddar or Gruyère
Freshly milled salt and pepper
4 tbsp milk

1. Preheat the oven to 180°C, Fan 165°C, Gas 4. Grease a shallow ovenproof dish with butter.

2. Peel and thinly slice the potatoes. Thinly slice the onion and finely chop or crush the garlic (if using). Finely chop the sage leaves. Grate the cheese and mix with the sage. Cut the butter into small pieces.

3. In the prepared dish, layer the potatoes, onion and garlic (if using) with about two-thirds of the cheese mixture, seasoning lightly as you go. Add the milk and dot the surface with the butter. Cover the dish securely with foil.

4. Put into the hot oven and cook for about 1¼ hours or until the potatoes are very soft when pierced with a knife.

5. Remove the foil and top the potatoes with the remaining cheese mixture. Increase the heat to 200°C, Fan 185°C, Gas 6 and cook for a further 10 minutes or until bubbling and golden on top.

Mint and Lemon Cannelloni in Tomato Sauce

Rustle up a quick dish of cannelloni – instead of making a sauce, use a carton of passata (sieved tomatoes) with added herbs. Serve with dressed green salad and maybe some warm Italian-style bread such as ciabatta.

Serves 2

1 small lemon
Small handful of mint leaves
50g/1¾ oz Parmesan cheese
Olive oil
250g carton ricotta cheese
Pinch of grated nutmeg
Freshly milled salt and pepper
6 fresh lasagne sheets
100ml/3½ fl oz vegetable stock
250ml/9 fl oz passata (sieved tomatoes) with basil

1.　Preheat the oven to 200°C, Fan 185°C, Gas 6.

2.　Finely grate the rind from the lemon. Finely chop the mint leaves. Finely grate the Parmesan cheese.

3.　Brush a shallow ovenproof dish with a little oil.

4.　Mix the ricotta cheese with two-thirds of the grated Parmesan and the lemon rind, mint and nutmeg. Season lightly with salt and pepper. Place a spoonful of the mixture onto a lasagne sheet and roll up. Repeat with the remaining cheese mixture and lasagne and arrange the rolls, side by side, in the prepared dish.

5.　Stir the stock into the passata and spoon the mixture over the top, making sure that the pasta is completely covered. Sprinkle the remaining Parmesan cheese over.

6.　Put into the hot oven and cook for about 30–40 minutes until piping hot and golden brown.

Pepper Halves filled with Smoked Trout

Peppers are delicious edible containers for fillings. We've used a cheese, trout and tomato mixture, packed with flavour.

Serves 1

2 spring onions
1 large red pepper
2 medium tomatoes
50g/1¾ oz hard cheese, such as Cheddar, Parmesan or
  Red Leicester
1 cooked, smoked trout fillet
1 tsp horseradish sauce
1 tbsp olive oil

1. Preheat the oven to 190°C, Fan 175°C, Gas 5.

2. Finely chop the spring onions. Cut the pepper in half vertically through the stalk. Remove the seeds but leave the stalk in place. Thinly slice the tomatoes. Finely grate the cheese.

3. Remove the skin from the trout and flake the fish, removing any bones.

4. In a small bowl, mix the onions, flaked fish and horseradish sauce.

5. Brush a little oil over the outside of each pepper half and put in a shallow ovenproof dish, skin side down.

6. Divide the fish mixture between the halves. Overlap the tomato slices on top and sprinkle with the cheese. Drizzle the remaining oil over the top.

7. Put into the hot oven and cook for 20 minutes until the peppers have softened and the tops are golden brown.

Salmon, Tomato and Olive Tart

For speed, buy a ready-made plain pastry case. Swap the salmon with tuna if you prefer. Serve with a salad of dressed mixed leaves.

Serves 2

4 spring onions
6 cherry tomatoes
1 tbsp capers
½ lemon
200g can salmon
2 medium eggs
142ml carton double cream
Freshly milled salt and pepper
20cm/8 inch cooked plain pastry case
Lemon wedges, to serve

1. Preheat the oven to 190°C, Fan 175°C, Gas 5.

2. Thinly slice the spring onions, quarter the tomatoes and roughly chop the capers. Finely grate the rind from the lemon. Drain the salmon and remove any large bones.

3. Lightly beat the eggs and stir in the cream, spring onions, lemon rind, capers and salmon. Season with salt and pepper.

4. Put the pastry case (still in its foil tray) on a baking sheet. Pour the egg mixture into the pastry and scatter the tomatoes over, pressing them gently just under the surface.

5. Put into the hot oven and cook for about 30 minutes or until set and golden brown.

6. Serve warm or at room temperature with lemon wedges for squeezing over.

Trout in a Foil Parcel

Also good with whole mackerel or skinless chicken breasts.

Serves 2

**Handful of mixed mushrooms, such as chestnut, oyster and
   shiitake**
1 small red onion
1 lemon
1 garlic clove
2 whole trout, gutted, heads on or off
Freshly milled salt and pepper
Sprigs of thyme
Oil
50g/1¾ oz couscous
Handful of baby spinach leaves
4 tbsp dry white wine, cider or apple juice
2 small pieces of butter

1. Preheat the oven to 200°C, Fan 185°C, Gas 6.
2. Clean and trim the mushrooms, halving them if large.
    Thinly slice the onion.
3. Thinly slice the lemon and the garlic clove. Wash the fish,
    inside and out, and dry well with kitchen paper. Season
    lightly, inside and out, and then fill their cavities with the
    lemon and garlic slices and a few sprigs of thyme.
4. Cut three large sheets of foil. Put two layers of foil on a
    baking sheet and brush the top surface with oil. Scrunch
    up the edges slightly (to prevent the ingredients from
    spilling out as you make up the parcel).
5. Spread the couscous in the centre of the foil and pile the
    spinach leaves and mushrooms on top. Lay the fish, side
    by side, on the vegetables and scatter the onion over.
    Drizzle with the wine, cider or apple juice and dot with the
    butter.
6. Brush a little oil over the remaining foil and place it, oiled
    side down, on top of the fish. Scrunch all the foil edges
    together to make a spacious but securely-sealed parcel.
    Put into the hot oven and cook for 25 minutes.
7. Tear open the parcel, carefully lift the trout onto warmed
    serving plates and spoon the vegetable-and-couscous
    mixture alongside.

Sticky Roast Chicken and Chips

Good eaten with the fingers while watching a video! Remember to serve up napkins too. Lining the roasting tin with some baking paper will save on washing up.

Serves 2

1 large baking potato
1 medium sweet potato
1 tbsp oil
A good pinch of ground cumin (optional)
Freshly milled salt and pepper
1 tbsp tomato ketchup
1 tbsp Worcestershire sauce
1 tbsp ready-made mustard
1 tbsp clear honey
4–6 chicken drumsticks

1. Preheat the oven to 200°C, Fan 185°C, Gas 6.

2. Scrub the potatoes and cut each into about eight wedges. In a food (freezer) bag or mixing bowl, toss the potato wedges with the oil and cumin (if using) until well coated. Spread them, in a single layer, in a shallow roasting tin and add a little seasoning if wished. Put into the hot oven and cook for 10 minutes.

3. Meanwhile, in the same bag or bowl, mix together the tomato ketchup, Worcestershire sauce, mustard and honey. Add the chicken and turn until well coated.

4. Add the chicken to the centre of the roasting tin, pushing the potatoes towards the sides.

5. Return to the hot oven and cook for a further 30 minutes, turning the chicken and potatoes at least once, or until the potatoes are cooked and golden brown and the chicken is cooked through – juices should run clear when pierced with a skewer or sharp knife.

6. Serve immediately.

Spatchcock Poussins

Poussins are young chickens. Very delicate, they can be used with gentle or strong flavours, and are perfect for smothering with this spicy curry-paste mixture. 'Spatchcock' means to flatten and open out; this reduces the cooking time. Instructions are given below but you could ask your butcher to do it for you. You will need 4 wooden or metal skewers. Serve with lots of vegetables.

Serves 2

1 shallot
1 lime
Small bunch of fresh coriander
1 tbsp mild curry paste
3 tbsp natural yogurt
Freshly milled salt and black pepper
2 poussins
2 tbsp oil

1. Preheat the oven to 200°C, Fan 185°C, Gas 6.

2. Chop the shallot very finely. Grate the rind from the lime, cut in half and squeeze the juice. Finely chop the coriander. Put all into a small bowl, add the curry paste, yogurt and seasoning and mix thoroughly to make a thick paste.

3. To spatchcock (flatten out) the poussins, cut each side of the backbone with strong scissors or poultry shears and discard the backbone. Turn the birds over, opening them out and pressing down to flatten them. Wipe or pat dry with kitchen paper.

4. With your fingers, loosen the skin, then push and spread the paste in the pocket beneath (or you could skip this bit and just spread the paste over the skin). To keep the poussins flat during cooking, push two skewers diagonally through them.

5. Put onto a baking sheet, drizzle with the oil and cover with foil.

6. Put into the hot oven and cook for 45–55 minutes until golden brown and cooked through (to check, insert a skewer into the thickest part of the thigh – the juices should run clear).

Baked Chicken Loaf

Takes on the shape of the dish it's cooked in. A flavourful savoury mix that is also suitable for making into meatballs or burgers. Serve thickly sliced with bread and pickles.

Serves 1

1 small onion
1 skinless boneless chicken breast
2 thick slices of white bread
2 sage leaves
150ml/¼ pint chicken stock
1 medium egg
2 tbsp chopped parsley
Freshly milled black pepper

1. Preheat the oven to 180°C, Fan 165°C, Gas 4.

2. Quarter the onion and roughly chop the chicken. With a food processor, coarsely chop the onion, chicken, bread and sage and tip into a mixing bowl.

3. Add the stock, egg, parsley and seasoning, mixing thoroughly.

4. Spoon the mixture into a small ovenproof dish and level the surface.

5. Cover, put into the hot oven and cook for 30–40 minutes until firm to the touch and the juices run clear.

Lamb in a Foil Packet

Loosely based on the Greek dish called Stifado, we have added some sliced potato to make a substantial meal. Though this is perfect for one, you could of course make as many packets as you have guests. Serve still in its foil.

Serves 1

2 tsp olive oil
1 medium potato
2 shallots
1 small garlic clove
1 medium tomato
2 lean lamb chops, such as loin
Pinch of ground cinnamon
Freshly milled salt and pepper
Sprig of oregano or a good pinch of dried oregano
1 tbsp dry white wine, vermouth or water

1. Preheat the oven to 190°C, Fan 175°C, Gas 5. Cut a large sheet of foil and brush with a little olive oil.

2. Scrub and thinly slice the potato. Peel and thinly slice the shallots. Finely chop or crush the garlic. Slice the tomato.

3. Lay the potato slices in overlapping circles on the oiled foil. Scatter the shallots and garlic over, followed by the tomato slices. Place the lamb chops on top of the vegetables, season with the cinnamon and a little salt and pepper, and add the oregano. Gather the foil up the sides, and then drizzle the wine, or vermouth or water, and the remaining olive oil, over the top. Scrunch the foil edges together to make a spacious but securely-sealed parcel.

4. Put the parcel on a baking sheet, put into the hot oven and cook for about 40 minutes until everything is cooked through and beginning to brown on the edges.

Braised Beef with Red Wine and Mushrooms

A complete meal in the oven. Serve with a glass of red wine and top the split jacket potato with butter or soured cream.

Serves 1

1 small red onion
2 medium carrots
1 small turnip
2 celery sticks
200g/7 oz beef topside, in one piece
2 tsp beef bouillon
150ml/¼ pint red wine or water
1 tsp Dijon mustard
Freshly milled salt and black pepper
1 tbsp oil
Sprig of thyme
1 bay leaf
1 large potato
6 button mushrooms
2 tsp plain flour

1. Preheat the oven to 160°C, Fan 145°C, Gas 3.
2. Chop the onion, carrots and turnip. Thickly slice the celery. Pat the beef dry with kitchen paper.
3. Pour 400ml/14 fl oz water into a measuring jug, stir in the bouillon, red wine, mustard and some seasoning.
4. Heat the oil in a flameproof casserole, add the beef and cook quickly for 2–3 minutes on all sides until browned. Lift out with a slotted spoon. Add the vegetables and cook, stirring occasionally for 5 minutes.
5. Remove from the heat. Put the beef on top of the vegetables, add the thyme and bay leaf and pour the liquid over. Cover with a tightly fitting lid, put in the hot oven and cook for 45 minutes.
6. Scrub the potato clean and prick all over with a fork. Place on the oven shelf next to the casserole and cook for a further 1 hour.
7. Trim, clean and halve the mushrooms. Put the flour in a small bowl and mix with a little cold water to make a smooth paste.
8. Remove the lid from the casserole and stir in the flour paste and mushrooms. Return, uncovered, to the hot oven and cook for a further 15 minutes.

Oxtail and Beer Casserole

A rustic, old-fashioned, and rather neglected dish that is very warming and comforting when the weather is chilly. Serve with jacket or mashed potatoes or rice.

Serves 2

1 medium onion
2 medium potatoes
2 large carrots
4 celery sticks
2 streaky bacon rashers
1 tbsp plain flour
Freshly milled salt and black pepper
500g/1 lb 2 oz oxtail pieces
2 bay leaves
2 sprigs of thyme
600ml/1 pint beef stock

1. Preheat the oven to 180°C, Fan 165°C, Gas 4.

2. Roughly chop the onion and potatoes. Thickly slice the carrots and celery. With scissors, trim the rind from the bacon and chop the bacon roughly.

3. In a large bowl, mix the flour with some seasoning. Pat the oxtail dry with kitchen paper and turn the pieces in the flour until well coated.

4. Layer the onion, carrots, celery, bacon and oxtail in a medium ovenproof casserole. Add the herbs, top with the potatoes and pour the stock over.

5. Cover, put in the hot oven and cook for 2–2¼ hours until the meat is tender.

6. Remove the cover and cook a further 15 minutes until the top is golden brown.

Bacon-Wrapped Venison Steak with Sweet Potato

Bacon keeps the mustard topped venison moist whilst it cooks alongside a delicious mix of sweet potatoes, carrot and courgette.

Serves 1

1 medium carrot
1 courgette
2 small sweet potatoes
1 venison steak
1 streaky bacon rasher
1 tbsp oil
1 tsp wholegrain mustard
2 tsp dried mixed herbs
Freshly milled black pepper

1. Preheat the oven to 190°C, Fan 175°C, Gas 5.

2. Trim and finely chop the carrot, courgette and sweet potatoes. Pat the venison dry with kitchen paper. Cut the bacon rasher in half.

3. Pour the oil into a bowl, add the vegetables and stir until coated. Tip into a small shallow roasting tin and spread out to give a thin layer.

4. Put the steak in the bowl and turn to coat it with any remaining oil. Spread the mustard over the top of the steak and cover with the bacon. Place on top of the vegetables in the roasting tin. Sprinkle the dried herbs and black pepper over the vegetables and steak.

5. Put into the hot oven and cook for 40 minutes or until the steak is cooked to your liking.

5

FAMILY EATS

Here are some really easy recipes, ideal for the whole family (as our families would certainly agree). Young and old alike can join in the fun by choosing their favourite flavours. Try a large personalised pizza topped with hand-picked ingredients arranged in rows, or some of the numerous fillings for jacket potatoes. Oven potato wedges are always popular – they can go with chicken nuggets, or be dunked into a favourite sauce or relish.

Hotpots are great family dishes, as they can be cooked longer than prescribed and come to no harm, and there is a novel idea for risotto cooked in the oven, so no need to stand and stir.

And there's more: an easy pie (leek, bacon and egg) with ready-made pastry; baked dishes, both vegetable-based and pasta (pasta shells in a savoury cheese sauce); and of course a weekend roast (slow-cooked shoulder of lamb). Weekend or weekday, whatever your situation, there's something here for everyone.

Jackets and Fillings

Pick your favourite filling from the list below.

Serves 1

1 large jacket potato
Freshly milled salt and black pepper
Butter (optional)
1 tbsp grated cheese (choose your favourite)

1. Preheat the oven to 200°C, Fan 185°C, Gas 6.

2. Scrub the potato and dry with kitchen paper. With a sharp knife cut a shallow cross in the top and push a metal skewer through the middle.

3. Put straight on the shelf in the hot oven and cook for 50 minutes to 1 hour or until soft and cooked through. (The cooking time will depend on the size of the potato.)

4. Carefully remove the skewer, slit open the potato at the cross and add a little seasoning, butter (if using) and cheese. Eat whilst hot.

To add a filling:
5. Slit the hot potato open and, with a spoon, scoop the soft potato into a bowl. Add your chosen filling (see below), mix well and spoon back into the potato skin. Alternatively, slit the potato open, place in a small ovenproof dish and spoon the filling on top. Return the potato to the hot oven and cook for a further 10 minutes until piping hot.

Fillings:

(Quantities for one potato)

Cream Cheese, Chives and Peanuts
2 tbsp cream cheese mixed with 1 tbsp freshly chopped chives and a few chopped unsalted peanuts.

Bacon, Mushroom and Tomato
In a frying pan on the hob, quickly cook 2 chopped rashers of streaky bacon with 4 chopped mushrooms for a few minutes until cooked. Add 2 halved cherry tomatoes.

Pesto, Feta and Olive
1 tbsp pesto mixed with 2 pitted-and-chopped black olives and
60g/2¼ oz crumbled feta cheese.

Prawns, Red Pimento and Spinach
A small handful of cooked, peeled prawns mixed with a little
chopped red pimento, 1 tsp lemon juice and a few small
spinach leaves.

See also Savoury Flavoured Butters (page 98) – these make
good toppings for jacket potatoes.

Herby Oven Chips

*Always tempting, yet only a small amount of oil is used. Leave the
skins on the potatoes or take them off – it's up to you. Serve with
any main meal or as a snack with mayonnaise or sauces.*

Serves 4–6

900g/2 lb potatoes
2 fresh rosemary sprigs
2 fresh thyme sprigs
Small bunch parsley
2 tbsp olive oil
3 tbsp chopped fresh herbs
Freshly milled salt and black pepper

1. Preheat the oven to 200°C, Fan 185°C, Gas 6.

2. Cut the potatoes into wedges slightly larger than an
    orange segment. Strip the leaves from the rosemary and
    thyme sprigs and, with the parsley, chop finely.

3. Pour the oil into a large bowl and stir in all the herbs. Add
    the potato wedges and, with two large spoons or your
    hands, mix until thoroughly coated.

4. Arrange the coated wedges in a single layer on one or two
    baking sheets. Season lightly with salt and pepper.

5. Put in the hot oven and cook for 30–40 minutes until
    golden brown and cooked through.

Potato and Celeriac Bake

Delicious hot or at room temperature. It's particularly good served alongside roast pork, grilled sausages, chops or burgers. With the addition of extra cheese or some chunks of cooked ham at the end of step 5, it becomes a complete meal needing only a salad garnish.

Serves 6

1 small onion
1 leek
4 garlic cloves
568ml carton double cream
Pinch of ground nutmeg
450g/1 lb potatoes
450g/1 lb celeriac
Freshly milled salt and pepper
About 100g/3½ oz hard cheese, such as mature Cheddar
  or Parmesan (optional)

1. Preheat the oven to 180°C, Fan 165°C, Gas 4.

2. Finely chop the onion, leek and garlic. Stir the chopped mixture into the cream and add the nutmeg. Leave to stand while you complete the next step.

3. Thinly slice the potatoes and celeriac.

4. Tip the cream mixture into a very large saucepan and bring just to the boil.

5. Add the potatoes and celeriac, reduce the heat slightly and cook for a few minutes until the cream has thickened slightly. Season with salt and pepper.

6. Tip the mixture into a large, shallow, ovenproof dish and, if using, scatter the cheese over the top.

7. Put into the hot oven and cook for about 45 minutes until the vegetables are very soft and the top is golden brown.

Leek and Mushroom Risotto

Oven-cooked risotto? It may not be traditional but it is certainly delicious. Use a risotto rice such as arborio or carnaroli.

Serves 4

2 medium leeks
1 garlic clove
175g/6 oz mixed mushrooms, such as chestnut, oyster, shiitake
2 tbsp olive oil
250g/9 oz risotto rice
150ml/¼ pint dry white wine
900ml/1½ pints vegetable or chicken stock or mixture of the two
Freshly milled salt and black pepper
3 tbsp freshly grated Parmesan cheese, plus extra for serving
25g/1 oz butter
2 tbsp freshly chopped parsley

1. Thinly slice the leeks. Finely chop or crush the garlic. Thickly slice the mushrooms.

2. Preheat the oven to 150°C, Fan 135°C, Gas 2.

3. Put the oil, leeks and garlic into a large flameproof casserole and cook over a medium heat for 5–10 minutes, stirring frequently, until soft but not browned. Add the rice and cook, stirring, for about 2 minutes. Stir in the mushrooms.

4. Add the wine to the rice mixture and cook over a medium heat, stirring, until it has been absorbed. Add the stock and, stirring, bring just to the boil.

5. Put into the hot oven and cook uncovered for 25–30 minutes, until the liquid has been absorbed and the rice is tender.

6. Season lightly and stir in the Parmesan cheese, butter and parsley. Serve topped with extra Parmesan.

Personalised Pizzas

Have fun with this family meal. Ask your friends or family for their requests for toppings, and then add them in sections. Serve it straight or with a mixed salad.

Serves 4–6

1 small red onion
6 button mushrooms
4 artichoke hearts
100g/3½ oz mozzarella cheese
100g/3½ oz mature Cheddar cheese
Few sprigs of fresh oregano
1 frankfurter sausage
4 salami slices
150ml/¼ pint passata (sieved tomatoes)
1 tbsp tomato purée
375g packet ready-rolled shortcrust pastry
Small handful of baby spinach leaves
1 tbsp olive oil
6 pitted olives

1. Preheat the oven to 200°C, Fan 185°C, Gas 6.

2. Thinly slice the onion. Clean, trim and thinly slice the mushrooms. Quarter the artichoke hearts. Tear the mozzarella cheese into small pieces and coarsely grate the Cheddar. Pull the leaves from the oregano sprigs.

3. Thinly slice the sausage and roughly chop the salami. In a small bowl, mix the passata with the tomato purée.

4. Unroll the pastry onto a baking sheet and with your fingers pinch the edge of the pastry all the way round to form a small lip. Spread the tomato mixture over the pastry and scatter the spinach leaves over. Arrange the onion, mushrooms, artichokes, sausage and salami in groups, rows or just randomly scattered over the pizza. Sprinkle the two cheeses and the oregano leaves over, drizzle with the oil and add the olives.

5. Put into the hot oven and cook for about 30–40 minutes until golden brown on the edges and cooked through.

Pasta Shells with Spinach and Basil

A useful family recipe meal, simple to make, filling and very tasty. Can be made in large quantities and assembled the day before. For endless variations use different pasta shapes each time it's cooked. Serve with a tomato and leaf salad.

Serves 4

350g/12 oz pasta shells
600ml/1 pint milk
50g/1¾ oz plain flour
50g/1¾ oz butter
Freshly milled salt and pepper
100g/3½ oz cooked chicken
70g/2½ oz cooked smoked ham
100g/3½ oz Cheshire cheese
Small handful of spinach leaves
Small handful of basil leaves

1. Preheat the oven to 190°C, Fan 175°C, Gas 5.

2. Cook the pasta shells in a large saucepan of fast-boiling water following the packet instructions. Drain and tip into a large ovenproof dish.

3. Meanwhile, make the sauce. Pour the milk into a medium saucepan and add the flour, butter and some seasoning. Over a medium heat, bring to the boil, stirring all the time, and cook for 2–3 minutes until thickened and smooth. Pour over the pasta.

4. Cut the chicken and ham into small bite-size pieces and crumble the cheese. Stir into the pasta with the spinach and basil leaves.

5. Cover, put into the hot oven and cook for 30–40 minutes until piping hot and golden brown on top.

Leek, Bacon and Egg Pie

The nutmeg is not essential in this recipe but it does add a subtle flavour. Instead of nutmeg, try mixing a little yeast extract into the milk for brushing the pastry top. Serve the pie in wedges with a mixed salad.

Serves 4–6

200g/7 oz lean back bacon rashers
250g/9 oz leeks
1 tbsp olive oil
40g/1½ oz plain flour
1 tsp vegetable bouillon powder
¼ tsp ground nutmeg (optional)
425ml/¾ pint milk, plus extra for brushing
Freshly milled salt and pepper
4 medium eggs
375g packet ready-rolled shortcrust pastry

1. With scissors, trim the rind from the bacon rashers and cut the bacon into thin strips. Thinly slice the leeks.
2. Preheat the oven to 190°C, Fan 175°C, Gas 5.
3. Put the oil and bacon into a saucepan and cook over a medium heat for about 5 minutes, stirring occasionally, until the bacon is golden brown.
4. Stir in the leeks, cover and cook over a medium heat for 5 minutes, stirring once or twice, until slightly softened.
5. Stir in the flour, vegetable bouillon and nutmeg (if using). Remove from the heat and gradually stir in the milk. Cook, stirring constantly, until the sauce comes to the boil and thickens. Season lightly.
6. Pour the sauce into a shallow ovenproof pie dish, about 25cm/10 inches in diameter. Make four wells in the sauce and break an egg into each.
7. Unroll the pastry and lay it over the dish, allowing the edges to hang over the sides. With scissors, roughly trim off the excess (you could use the off-cuts to decorate the top of the pie – make leaves or roll into thin strips to make alphabet letters). Brush the top of the pastry with milk and make a small slit in the centre (to let out the steam).
8. Put into the hot oven and cook for about 40 minutes until golden brown.

Roasted Vegetables with Sausages

*Always a favourite – butcher's sausages, potatoes, courgettes,
carrots and peppers all cooked together in one large roasting tin.
Serve with lots of salad, pickles and sauces.*

Serves 4–6

600g/1 lb 5 oz potatoes
3 medium courgettes
3 medium carrots
2 red peppers
2 garlic bulbs
6 beefsteak tomatoes
Small bunch of parsley
2 tbsp olive oil
Freshly milled salt and pepper
10 butcher's sausages
A few rosemary and thyme sprigs

1. Preheat the oven to 200°C, Fan 185°C, Gas 6.

2. Scrub the potatoes thoroughly and cut into large bite-size
    pieces. Cut the courgettes and carrots into large chunks.
    Halve the peppers, remove the seeds and stalk and cut
    each piece in half. Slice the whole garlic bulbs and the
    tomatoes in half across the middle. Finely chop the parsley.

3. Pour the oil into a large bowl, stir in the parsley and some
    seasoning. Add the potatoes, courgettes, carrots and
    peppers and, with two large spoons or your hands, mix
    until thoroughly coated. Tip into a large roasting tin,
    spreading them to make a shallow layer.

4. Rub the cut surfaces of the garlic and tomatoes in the
    juices left in the bowl. Cut the sausages in half across the
    middle.

5. Add the garlic and sausages to the vegetables. Holding
    the sprigs of herbs over the dish, tear them apart, letting
    the pieces fall into the tin.

6. Put into the hot oven and cook for about 25–35 minutes,
    turning once or twice, until the sausages are cooked
    through and the vegetables are golden brown. Add the
    tomatoes for the final 5 minutes.

Chicken Nuggets

Guaranteed to please! Serve them with salad, baked jacket potatoes or wedges; or just as they are with your favourite sauce or chutney for dipping. Leave them to cool and they are ideal for buffets, picnics and packed lunches.

Serves 4

4 boneless, skinless chicken breasts
1 large egg
1 tbsp olive oil
4 slices of white bread
2 tbsp cornmeal (polenta)
2 tbsp freshly chopped herbs (thyme, oregano, mint) or
  1 tbsp dried herbs
Freshly milled salt and black pepper

1. Cut each chicken breast into three or four pieces. Break the egg into a shallow dish and beat lightly with the oil. Using a coarse grater, grate the bread to make small crumbs (or use a processor). Put them into a shallow dish and mix in the cornmeal, herbs and seasoning.

2. Put a large baking sheet into the oven and preheat to 190°C, Fan 175°C, Gas 5.

3. Using tongs or two forks, dip each chicken piece into the egg, allowing excess egg to drip off, then coat with the herby crumbs. Place on a sheet of baking paper. Repeat using the remaining chicken, egg and crumbs.

4. Slide the chicken (still on its baking paper) onto the hot baking sheet. If any of the pieces are touching, nudge them slightly away from each other. Put into the hot oven and cook for 15–20 minutes until crisp, golden brown and cooked through.

5. Serve hot or cold.

Chicken and Mushroom Casserole with Herb Dumplings

Dumplings make a quick and easy addition.

Serves 4–6

1 large onion
4 celery sticks
250g/9 oz chestnut mushrooms
4 chicken thighs and legs
Oil
2 tbsp plain flour
600ml/1 pint chicken stock
1 tbsp lemon juice
4 sage leaves
Freshly milled salt and pepper
200g/7 oz self-raising flour
100g/3½ oz butter
1 tbsp chopped parsley
Flour, for dusting

1. Thinly slice the onion and celery. Clean, trim and quarter the mushrooms. Pat the chicken dry with kitchen paper. Heat a little oil in a large flameproof casserole, add the chicken pieces in small batches, browning quickly on all sides and lifting out of the pan.

2. Add the onion and celery to the pan and cook for about 5 minutes, stirring occasionally, until softened. Return the chicken to the pan and stir in the plain flour. Stir in the mushrooms, stock, lemon juice, sage leaves and a little seasoning. Heat until almost boiling.

3. Cover, put into the oven and cook at 160°C, Fan 145°C, Gas 3 for about 1½ hours until the chicken is cooked through.

4. Meanwhile, make the dumplings. Tip the self-raising flour into a large bowl, add the butter and parsley, then with a fork mix it all together until like crumbs. Using a knife or hand, gradually mix in 3–4 tbsp cold water, a little at a time, mixing until it forms a soft dough. Cut into 8 portions and with floured hands roll into balls.

5. Lift the casserole from the oven, remove the lid and arrange the dumplings on the top. Cover, return to the oven and cook a further 15–20 minutes until the dumplings are risen, cooked and golden.

Lamb Hotpot

A traditional dish that has become fashionable again. If time allows, brown the lamb in a little olive oil on the hob before layering up the casserole and putting it in the oven – the extra flavour will be worth the effort.

Serves 4–6

8–12 lean, middle neck lamb chops
2 large leeks
2 medium carrots
1kg/2¼ lb potatoes
Freshly milled salt and black pepper
1 tbsp fresh thyme leaves or 1 tsp dried
600ml/1 pint lamb or vegetable stock
25g/1 oz butter

1. Trim any excess fat from the lamb chops. Slice the leeks and carrots. Thinly slice the potatoes.

2. Arrange one third of the potatoes in a large ovenproof casserole, seasoning lightly with salt, pepper and thyme. Lay 4–6 chops on top with half the leeks and carrots. Repeat with a second layer of potatoes, seasoning, thyme, chops, leeks and carrots. Arrange the remaining potatoes in overlapping circles on top and pour the stock over. Melt the butter and brush it over the potatoes.

3. Cover, put into the oven and cook at 150°C, Fan 135°C, Gas 2 for about 2 hours.

4. Remove the cover, increase the oven temperature to 220°C, Fan 205°C, Gas 7 and continue cooking for about 30 minutes or until the potatoes are crisp and deep golden brown.

Slow-Cooked Lamb in Tomatoes

The lamb sits in a thick tomato sauce, cooking very gently until it becomes meltingly tender – soft enough to pull apart with a fork. If you have the time, it's worth browning the lamb on the hob before putting it into the oven. Serve with rice or mash and stir-fried vegetables or salad.

Serves 6

2 onions
4 celery sticks
Boned shoulder of lamb, weighing about 1.5–2kg/3¼–4½ lb
Freshly milled salt and black pepper
6–8 garlic cloves
Leaves from a good bunch of fresh rosemary
Olive oil
150ml/¼ pint dry red wine
Two 400g cans chopped tomatoes

1. Finely chop the onions and celery.

2. With a sharp knife, make several slashes in the lamb and season with salt and pepper.

3. Finely chop the garlic and rosemary, mixing them together to make a rough paste (for best results, pound the chopped garlic and rosemary with pestle and mortar). Push the mixture into the slashes in the lamb.

4. If time allows, heat some olive oil in a sturdy roasting tin, add the lamb and brown it quickly on all sides.

5. Add the onions, celery and wine. Bring to the boil and bubble until the wine has reduced by about half.

6. Add both cans of tomatoes and 300ml/½ pint water. Bring just to the boil then cover securely with a large sheet of foil.

7. Put into the oven and cook at 110–130°C, Fan 110–115°C, Gas ¼-½ for about 4½ hours until very tender.

Beef in Ale with Mustard Toasts

A favourite with Annette's family. She serves it with green salad or stir-fried vegetables.

Serves 6

2 large onions
4 bacon rashers
1kg/2¼ lb lean stewing beef
2 tbsp oil
2 tbsp plain flour
500ml/18 fl oz brown ale
300ml/½ pint beef or vegetable stock
1 tbsp tomato purée
1 tsp sugar
2 tbsp fresh thyme leaves or 2 tsp dried
Freshly milled salt and black pepper
Dijon, wholegrain or English mustard
12 slices of French bread

1. Halve and slice the onions. With scissors, trim the rind from the bacon rashers and cut the bacon into small pieces. Cut the beef into large chunks.
2. Heat the oil in a large flameproof casserole, add the bacon and cook quickly for a few minutes, stirring occasionally, until golden brown. Lift out with a slotted spoon.
3. Add the beef, in small batches, browning quickly on all sides and lifting out of the pan.
4. Add the onions to the pan and cook for about 5 minutes, stirring occasionally, until golden. Return the bacon to the pan and stir in the flour. Stir in the ale, stock, tomato purée, sugar, thyme and a little seasoning. Add the beef and its juices. Heat until the gentlest of bubbles rise to the surface of the liquid (do not allow it to boil).
5. Cover, put into the oven and cook at 150°C, Fan 135°C, Gas 2 for about 2½ hours until the beef is tender.
6. Spread some mustard on one side of each bread slice and arrange them, mustard-side down, on top of the hot beef (you may like to spoon some of the juices over the top of the bread). Return the casserole to the oven, uncovered, for a further 30 minutes until the bread is crusty.

6

FEASTS FOR FRIENDS

For your dearest friends, you want it to be something a bit special. These are the kinds of special dishes we always have in mind when our thoughts turn to entertaining. A classy casserole of beef in red wine, a tagine of lamb, braised pheasant or cassoulet – all of them set the scene for a wonderful convivial evening.

Though designed to be impressive (and it's nice to create a bit of an impression from time to time), all the recipes in this section are deceptively simple to make. The secret is that they are quick to prepare and long and slow in the cooking. An unusual fish pie uses scrunched-up sheets of filo pastry for its lid, a whole fish is served with parcels of potato and beetroot, and there are a couple of pork roasts as well as finger-licking sticky spare-ribs.

Use a dash of alcohol and good quality ingredients – a little more expensive than usual – and then you have the recipe for a memorable shared feast.

baby onions

Crab and Prawn Tart

A tempting fish dish made using two types of pastry, both ready-made. A shortcrust pastry case filled with crab and prawns is topped with tissue-thin filo pastry scrunched over the top. Serve with green salad and lemon wedges to squeeze over.

Serves 6

1 medium courgette
2 medium eggs
150ml/¼ pint milk
250g/9 oz curd cheese
200g/7 oz crabmeat
200g/7 oz cooked, peeled prawns
1 tbsp freshly chopped dill
1 tbsp lemon juice
Freshly milled black pepper
18 cm/7 inch ready-made uncooked pastry case
2 sheets filo pastry
2 tsp melted butter
Parmesan shavings

1. Preheat the oven to 200°C, Fan 185°C, Gas 6.

2. Trim the courgette and chop finely.

3. Break the eggs into a large bowl and stir in the milk and curd cheese until smooth. Mix in the courgette, crabmeat, prawns, dill, lemon juice and black pepper.

4. Put the pastry case (still in its foil container) on a baking sheet and spoon in the filling.

5. Brush each sheet of filo pastry with melted butter, then fold and scrunch the pastry and arrange the pieces on top of the filling, to make a top for the pie.

6. Put into the hot oven and cook for 35–40 minutes until the tart is cooked and golden.

7. Scatter Parmesan flakes over the top, cut into wedges and serve.

Whole Roast Fish with Beetroots, Potatoes and Garlic

First a foil parcel of beetroots goes into the oven. After an hour the potatoes are added – also in foil. When the beetroots come out, the fish goes in. By the time the fish is cooked, the potatoes are tender and the beetroots are cool enough to peel and serve.

Serves 6

3 garlic cloves
12 medium beetroots
About 6 sprigs of fresh thyme
Freshly milled salt and black pepper
3 tbsp olive oil
About 24 small potatoes
Large whole fish, such as sea bass or salmon, weighing
about 1.3kg/3 lb
Lemon wedges to serve

1. Preheat the oven to 180°C, Fan 165°C, Gas 4.
2. Roughly chop the garlic. Scrub and drain the beetroots, then put them onto a large square of foil with a few sprigs of thyme, half the garlic and a little salt and pepper. Drizzle 1 tbsp olive oil over. Gather up the foil, seal the parcel securely and place on a baking sheet. Put into the hot oven and cook for 1 hour.
3. Meanwhile, halve the potatoes and put them onto another large square of foil with a few sprigs of thyme, the remaining garlic and a little salt and pepper. Drizzle with 1 tbsp olive oil. Gather up the foil, seal the parcel securely and place on a baking sheet.
4. When the beetroots have had their hour's cooking, put the parcel of potatoes into the hot oven (with the beetroots) and cook for 1 hour.
5. Meanwhile, put the fish in a shallow ovenproof dish and drizzle with the remaining 1 tbsp olive oil.
6. Remove the parcel of beetroots and put the fish into the hot oven (with the potatoes). Cook for about 45 minutes or until the fish is just cooked.
7. Just before serving, remove and discard the skin from the beetroots and serve with the fish and potatoes and their juices.

Hot Smoked Salmon and Prawns in Filo Pastry

Serves 6–8 as a starter, 4 as a main course

1 small red onion
Small bunch of dill
1 lime
1 medium red pepper
4 cooked asparagus spears, fresh, frozen or canned
60g/2¼ oz butter
250g/9 oz smoked salmon slices
250g/9 oz cooked shelled prawns, thawed if frozen
200g/7 oz light cream cheese
2 tbsp tomato purée
Freshly milled black pepper
8 sheets filo pastry, thawed if frozen

1. Preheat the oven to 190°C, Fan 175°C, Gas 5.
2. Finely chop the onion and the dill. Finely grate the rind from half the lime, cut in half and squeeze the juice from the whole lime. Cut the pepper in half, remove and discard the seeds and stalk, and chop finely. Cut the asparagus spears into short lengths.
3. Melt the butter (on the hob or in the microwave) and cool. Cut the salmon into finger-length strips. Dry the prawns on kitchen paper.
4. Put the cream cheese in a large bowl and stir in the onion, dill, lime rind and juice, tomato purée and a little black pepper, mixing thoroughly.
5. Unroll the filo pastry, keeping it covered with cling film until needed. Put a pastry sheet onto a large baking sheet and brush with a little melted butter. Repeat with the remaining pastry.
6. Spread the cream cheese mixture over the pastry, keeping it clear of the edges. Put the red pepper down the length of the pastry and top with the asparagus, salmon and prawns.
7. Fold the two long sides over the filling to just overlap. Press gently to seal. Carefully turn the pastry roll over, seam side down. Brush with melted butter and, with a sharp knife, make a few diagonal slashes in the pastry top. Put into the hot oven and cook for 30–40 minutes until cooked, crisp and golden. Serve sliced.

Watercress and Lemon Filled Salmon with Vermouth

Perfect for those special occasions, salmon fillets are sandwiched with a delicious lemon, watercress, parsley and courgette filling. No bones to bother about, just slice and serve. Choose two salmon fillets with a similar shape.

Serves 6

1 lemon
1 bunch watercress
Small bunch parsley
2 small courgettes
Freshly milled salt and black pepper
2 salmon fillets, total weight about 1kg/2¼ lb
3 tbsp dry white vermouth
1 tbsp olive oil
Lemon wedges to serve

1. Preheat the oven to 190°C, Fan 175°C, Gas 5.

2. Finely grate the rind from the lemon and squeeze out the juice. Strip the watercress leaves from the thick stalks and chop the leaves finely together with the parsley. Trim and coarsely grate the courgettes.

3. In a small bowl mix together the watercress, parsley, courgettes and lemon rind and juice. Season with a little salt and pepper.

4. Wash the salmon fillets and dry with kitchen paper. Put one fillet, skin side down, on a clean surface. Press the watercress mixture over the surface and cover with the second fillet, skin side uppermost. Tie the fish parcel at intervals with thin string.

5. Lift the parcel into a shallow ovenproof dish. Pour the vermouth over and drizzle with the olive oil.

6. Put into the hot oven and cook for about 35 minutes or until the salmon is just cooked.

7. Just before serving, remove the string and cut the salmon into thick slices. Serve with any juices spooned over and lemon wedges on the side.

Chilli Chicken

This is the dish on the front cover of this book. It's colourful and simple to prepare. Serve with crusty bread.

Serves 4

2 small red onions
1 red pepper
1 orange pepper
2 medium courgettes
175g/6 oz mixed mushrooms
4 chicken portions, or 4 thighs and 4 drumsticks
2 tbsp olive oil
600ml/1 pint chicken stock
1 tsp mild chilli powder
3 bay leaves
Freshly milled salt and pepper
1 tbsp chopped fresh parsley

1. Preheat the oven to 180°C, Fan 165°C, Gas 4.

2. Cut each red onion into 6 wedges. Cut the peppers in half, remove and discard the seeds and stalks, and slice thickly. Trim and roughly slice the courgettes. Clean and trim the mushrooms, cutting them in half if large. If using chicken portions, cut each one into two (to make thighs and drumsticks).

3. Heat the oil in a large flameproof casserole, add the chicken pieces and brown quickly all over. Lift out.

4. Add the onions, peppers, courgettes and mushrooms and cook quickly for a few minutes, stirring occasionally, until golden. Stir in the stock, chilli powder and bay leaves. Add the chicken and its juices. Bring just to the boil.

5. Cover, put into the hot oven and cook for 1–1¼ hours or until the chicken is cooked through, removing the cover for the final 15 minutes.

6. Season if necessary, scatter the parsley over and serve immediately.

Pheasant Braised with Onions and Chestnuts

Serves 4–6

100g/3½ oz lean, streaky bacon rashers
2 celery sticks
1 small orange
1 tbsp oil
25g/1 oz butter
2 oven-ready pheasants
8–12 baby onions or shallots
240g can chestnuts
1 tbsp wine vinegar
2 tsp brown sugar
150ml/¼ pint red wine
150ml/¼ pint chicken stock
Freshly milled salt and black pepper
1 tbsp cornflour
Freshly chopped parsley to serve

1. With scissors, trim the rind from the bacon and cut the bacon into small pieces. Thinly slice the celery. With a vegetable peeler, thinly pare the rind from the orange in wide strips, making sure no white pith is attached. Halve the orange and squeeze the juice.
2. Preheat the oven to 160°C, Fan 145°C, Gas 3.
3. Heat the oil and butter in a flameproof casserole, large enough to hold the pheasants side by side. Brown them quickly in the oil and butter on all sides and lift out.
4. Add the bacon, celery, whole onions or shallots and chestnuts to the casserole and cook over a medium heat for about 5 minutes or until beginning to brown.
5. Stir in the vinegar and bubble briefly, and then add the sugar, wine, stock, orange rind and juice, and seasoning. Bring just to the boil and add the browned pheasants and their juices.
6. Cover, cook in the oven for 1½ hours until the pheasants are tender, lift onto a serving plate and keep warm.
7. Mix the cornflour with a little cold water to make a smooth paste. Whisk in a couple of spoonfuls of the hot stock, then stir the mixture into the casserole. Cook over a medium heat, stirring, until the sauce comes to the boil and thickens. Adjust the seasoning if necessary. Serve the sauce with the pheasant, all sprinkled liberally with parsley.

Easy Cassoulet

Serve this flavour-packed cassoulet with plenty of hot garlic bread (page 100). Your favourite butcher's sausages could be used instead of smoked sausage – just remove the skins and cut the sausage meat into small chunks.

Serves 8

8 skinless, boneless chicken thighs
250g/9 oz thick back bacon rashers
2 large onions
4 celery stalks
3 garlic cloves
Two 400g cans white beans, such as haricot
2 tbsp olive oil
450ml/¾ pint chicken or vegetable stock
2 tbsp black treacle
2 tbsp wholegrain mustard
Freshly milled black pepper
250g/9 oz smoked sausage
Chopped fresh parsley, to serve

1. Cut each chicken thigh into about 3 pieces. With scissors, trim the rind from the bacon and cut the bacon into small pieces. Chop the onions and thinly slice the celery. Finely chop or crush the garlic. Drain the beans.
2. Preheat the oven to 150°C, Fan 135°C, Gas 2.
3. Heat a large non-stick frying pan, add the bacon and cook on a medium heat for about 5 minutes, stirring occasionally, until golden brown and some of the fat has run out. With a slotted spoon, transfer the bacon to a large ovenproof casserole.
4. Add the oil to the frying pan, stir in the onions, celery and garlic and cook for a few minutes, until beginning to brown. Stir in the stock, treacle, mustard, chicken and beans. Season with pepper and bring just to the boil. Pour the mixture over the bacon in the casserole.
5. Cover, put into the hot oven and cook for 1–1¼ hours until the vegetables and chicken are tender.
6. Remove the skin from the sausage and cut into thick slices. Stir into the casserole, cover and continue cooking for 10–15 minutes.
7. Serve sprinkled with plenty of parsley.

Beef in Red Wine with Baby Onions and Mushrooms

Browning the meat first gives good flavour and colour. If time is too short, put all the ingredients into the casserole, except the flour, and heat on the hob until the gentlest of bubbles rise to the surface (don't allow it to boil). Then cover and cook as in step 4. At the start of step 6 blend the flour with a little cold water to make a smooth paste, stir in some of the hot liquid from the beef, then stir into the casserole.

Serves 6

200g/7 oz lean streaky bacon rashers
1kg/2¼ lb lean braising steak
2 garlic cloves
2 tbsp oil
2 tbsp plain flour
300ml/½ pint red wine such as burgundy
150ml/¼ pint beef or vegetable stock
2 tbsp fresh thyme leaves or 2 tsp dried
Freshly milled salt and black pepper
25g/1 oz butter
18 baby onions or shallots
150g/5½ oz button mushrooms

1. With scissors, trim the rind from the bacon and cut the bacon into small pieces. Cut the beef into large chunks. Finely chop or crush the garlic.
2. Heat the oil in a flameproof casserole, add the bacon and cook over a medium heat for about 5 minutes, stirring occasionally, until golden brown. Lift out with a slotted spoon. Add the beef, in small batches, browning quickly on all sides and lifting out of the pan.
3. Return the bacon to the pan and stir in the garlic and flour. Stir in the wine, stock, thyme and a little seasoning. Add the beef and its juices. Heat until the gentlest of bubbles rise to the surface of the liquid (do not allow it to boil).
4. Cover, put into the oven and cook at 150°C, Fan 135°C, Gas 2 for about 2½ hours.
5. Melt the butter in a frying pan, add the onions or shallots and cook until golden brown. Lift out. Add the mushrooms to the hot pan and brown quickly.
6. Stir the browned onions and mushrooms into the casserole, cover and cook for a further 30 minutes.

Lamb and Olive Tajine

A Tajine is an earthenware cooking pot traditionally used in Morocco to make stews, usually of meat or poultry, with vegetables, olives, turmeric and spices.

Serves 4–6

700g/1 lb 9 oz boneless lamb
2 medium onions
2 garlic cloves
1 lemon
2 tbsp oil
½ tsp ground turmeric
500ml/18 fl oz chicken or vegetable stock
4 tbsp tomato purée
2 tsp caraway seeds
1 tbsp plain flour
12 green or black pitted olives
Freshly milled salt and black pepper

1. Trim any excess fat from the lamb and cut into large, bite-size chunks. Thinly slice the onions and finely chop or crush the garlic. Grate the rind from the lemon, cut in half and squeeze the juice.

2. Heat the oil in a flameproof casserole, add the lamb in small batches and cook for about 5 minutes, browning quickly on all sides. Lift out with a slotted spoon.

3. Add the onions to the casserole and cook for about 5 minutes until lightly browned, stirring occasionally. Return the lamb to the casserole and stir in the garlic, lemon rind and juice, turmeric, stock, tomato purée and caraway seeds. Heat until the gentlest of bubbles rise to the surface of the liquid (do not allow it to boil).

4. Cover, put in the oven and cook at 160°C, Fan 145°C, Gas 3 for about 1½ hours until the meat is very tender.

5. Blend the flour with a little cold water to make a smooth paste. Stir into the casserole and add the olives.

6. Cover, return to the hot oven and cook for a further 15 minutes before seasoning if necessary.

Lamb Shanks with Rosemary and Thyme

Serve with rice or mashed potatoes and parsnips.

Serves 4

2 large onions
2 large garlic cloves
2 red peppers
4 lamb shanks
1 tbsp olive oil
450ml/¾ pint lamb or chicken stock
150ml/¼ pint passata (sieved tomatoes)
4 sprigs of fresh rosemary
4 sprigs of fresh thyme
1 tbsp cornflour
2 tbsp redcurrant jelly
1 tbsp freshly chopped parsley
Freshly milled salt and black pepper

1. Chop the onions and finely chop or crush the garlic. Cut the peppers in half, remove and discard the seeds and stalks, and slice thinly. Trim excess fat from the lamb.
2. Heat the oil in a large non-stick frying pan. Add the lamb shanks, two at a time. Cook quickly, turning with tongs, until golden brown all over. With a slotted spoon, transfer the lamb to a large ovenproof casserole.
3. Add the onions and garlic to the frying pan, stir in the peppers and cook for a few minutes, stirring occasionally, until beginning to brown. Stir in the stock, passata, rosemary and thyme. Bring just to the boil and pour over the lamb in the casserole.
4. Cover, put in the oven and cook at 160°C, Fan 145°C, Gas 3 for 1¼-1½ hours until the lamb is cooked through and so tender that it almost falls off the bone.
5. Remove from the oven and, with a slotted spoon, lift the lamb onto a large plate, cover and keep warm.
6. Put the casserole on the hob over a medium heat. Lift out and discard the woody rosemary and thyme stalks. In a small bowl, mix the cornflour with a little water to make a smooth paste and stir into the casserole with the redcurrant jelly and parsley. Stirring continuously, bring to the boil and cook for 2–3 minutes until thickened, seasoning if necessary.
7. Serve the lamb with the sauce spooned over.

Fruity Stuffed Pork Wrapped in Pancetta

Impress your friends with this prune, apricot-and-almond-filled tender pork wrapped in pancetta. Don't tell them how easy it is to prepare.

Serves 4–6

2 shallots
100g/3½ oz oyster mushrooms
6 pitted prunes
6 blanched almonds
6 ready-to-eat dried apricots
2 tbsp dry cider, dry white vermouth or vegetable stock
1 tbsp freshly chopped parsley
1 tbsp olive oil
Freshly milled black pepper
600g/1 lb 5 oz pork tenderloin, in one or two pieces
6 slices of pancetta

1. Preheat the oven to 190°C, Fan 175°C, Gas 5.
2. Finely chop the shallots. Clean, trim and finely chop the mushrooms. Cut a slit in each prune and insert a whole almond. Finely chop the apricots.
3. In a large bowl mix together the shallots, mushrooms, apricots, cider, parsley and 1 tsp of the oil. Season with a little pepper.
4. Pat the pork dry with kitchen paper. Cut a slit along the length, without cutting all the way through, and open out the pork.
5. Put the prunes in a line down the middle. Spoon the mushroom mixture over and press it down firmly. Fold the meat over the filling and wrap the pancetta slices over the meat. Tie with string at intervals, to secure it during cooking.
6. Lift the stuffed pork into a roasting tin, brush with oil and cover with foil.
7. Put into the hot oven and cook for 1–1¼ hours until cooked through, removing the foil for the final 20 minutes to allow it to brown a little.
8. Remove from the oven, cover and keep warm for 15 minutes before carving into thick slices and serving.

Glazed Spare Ribs

Be prepared for sticky fingers all round. Short meaty ribs will cook more evenly. If time allows, leave the uncooked pork to marinate in the sauce for an hour or two before cooking. Serve just as they are or with rice, couscous or salad.

Serves 4–6

1 medium onion
1 garlic clove
4 tbsp tomato ketchup
4 tbsp Worcestershire sauce
1 tbsp vinegar, malt or wine
1 tbsp soft brown sugar
1 tbsp mustard
1kg/2¼ lb lean pork spare ribs

1. Preheat the oven to 160°C, Fan 145°C, Gas 3.

2. Finely chop or grate the onion. Finely chop or crush the garlic.

3. Put the onion and garlic in a large bowl and stir in the tomato ketchup, Worcestershire sauce, vinegar, sugar and mustard. Add the pork ribs, turning them in the sauce until well coated.

4. Arrange the ribs in a single layer in a shallow ovenproof dish and drizzle the sauce over. Cover the dish securely with foil.

5. Put into the hot oven and cook for 1½ hours – if possible, turn them over after the first hour, though this is not essential.

6. Remove the foil and increase the oven heat to 200°C, Fan 185°C, Gas 6. Continue cooking, uncovered, for a further 20–30 minutes until the pork is crisp on the edges, browned and tender.

Next-Day Leg of Pork

Put the pork in the oven and forget about it until the next day, when it will be so tender and moist that it can be pulled off the bone. It's great for feeding a crowd. Serve it simply, with its generous pan juices spooned over and vegetables alongside, or thickly sliced and stuffed into fresh bread rolls with crisp salad leaves. Make sure you buy leg of pork with the bone in, and ask your butcher to score the pork rind really well.

Serves 8–15 or even more

2 small lemons
4 tbsp freshly milled salt
1 tbsp freshly milled pepper
1 tbsp dried thyme or 2–3 tbsp fresh leaves
Leg of pork weighing about 2.2–4.5kg/5–10 lb
1 head of garlic (8–10 cloves)
**350ml/12 fl oz dry white wine or a mixture of wine and
    apple juice**

1. Preheat the oven to 250°C, Fan 235°C, Gas 9.
2. Finely grate the rind from the lemons and mix it with the salt, pepper and thyme. Rub the mixture over the pork rind, pushing it into the scored lines.
3. Halve the garlic cloves. With a sharp knife, make several small, deep cuts in the pork and push the garlic pieces into the meat. Put the joint in a large, deep roasting tin.
4. Halve the lemons, squeeze the juice and drizzle it over the pork. Pour the wine into the tin.
5. Put into the hot oven and cook for 20–30 minutes or until the skin crackles and crisps.
6. Reduce the oven heat to 100°C, Fan 100°C, Gas ¼.
7. Pour 300ml/½ pint cold water around the pork and cover the tin with a generous sheet of greaseproof paper and then foil. Scrunch the paper and foil around the edges of the tin to seal it securely. Put into the hot oven and cook for 12–14 hours (2.2kg/5 lb) or 18–24 hours (4.5kg/10 lb) until the meat is very tender.
8. To crisp up the skin, remove the paper and foil, increase the oven heat to 250°C, Fan 235°C, Gas 9 and cook for a further 15–20 minutes.

7

FAST TOPPINGS & SIDELINES

Here are all the extras, a miscellany of recipe ideas to give sparkle and variety to your main meals. Feel free to add these toppings and sidelines to other dishes you find in this book. Like spontaneous gestures, they can surprise and stimulate, and reflect the mood of the moment. The sidelines are for serving alongside other dishes; the toppings can often supply crispness at the last moment.

Try the traditional-style breads, soda bread, savoury scones, garlic and herb breads, all quick to make, or the croûtons for crunchiness. Stir pesto into soups for an instant flavour hit, or spread it on toast. Gremolata as a topping gives a burst of lemon freshness and herbs.

Cheese and Walnut Toasts (on page 96) can be served just as they are with drinks, on top of a casserole, or floating on bowls of soup. Also try mini mustard and parsley muffins, with drinks or with a casserole; root vegetable crisps (beetroot, parsnip, etc); sprouted beans, seeds and grains as a salad on the side; spiced seeds and nuts; or oat and cereal crunch, a crumble-type topping for casseroles. Plus melon and chicory salad, salsa and flavoured butters. The possibilities are just about endless.

Croûton Toppings

Ideal for adding a crunch to soups and casseroles. Scatter them on top just before serving. Here are some ideas.

- The simplest method is to toast some bread (in the toaster or under a hot grill) and, while it is still hot, cut into cubes. Add a hint of garlic by rubbing the hot toast with the cut side of a garlic clove first.

- Spread garlic or herb butter over your chosen bread slices before toasting them under a hot grill and cutting into shapes.

- For extra-crispy croûtons, cut the crusts off the bread slices and cut the bread into small cubes. Heat some butter and/or oil in a shallow pan on the hob until hot. Add the bread cubes and cook over a medium heat, occasionally stirring gently, until crisp and golden brown. Drain on kitchen paper and serve. These croûtons can be cooled and kept in a sealed container for up to one week.

- Sometimes it's nice to have larger toasts, something that makes an almost-instant alternative to potatoes, rice or pasta. Just toast thick slices of French bread and spread them with garlic butter, pesto or mustard (add some grated hard cheese or slices of goats' cheese too if you like). Pop them back under the grill until golden and bubbling. Delicious floated on a bowl of soup or on a casserole. See also Cheese and Walnut Toasts on page 96 and Beef in Ale with Mustard Toasts on page 78.

Oat and Cereal Crunch

A crunchy mix, you may be surprised to see breakfast cereals here. Cereals have a neutral quality and absorb whichever flavouring you add to them. Here we've made them spicy rather than sweet. Serve scattered over vegetables, rice, pasta, casseroles, and salads.

Serves 4–6

2 tbsp olive oil
2 tbsp light soy sauce
1 tbsp cider vinegar
1 tbsp soft brown sugar
Freshly milled salt and pepper
200g/7 oz jumbo porridge oats
200g/7 oz sugar-free puffed wheat
100g/3½ oz sesame seeds

1. Preheat the oven to 190°C, Fan 175°C, Gas 5.

2. In a large bowl, mix together the oil, soy sauce, cider vinegar, brown sugar and seasoning. Add the oats, puffed wheat and sesame seeds and mix until thoroughly coated. Spread thinly over two or three baking sheets.

3. Put into the hot oven and cook for 10 minutes or until hot and lightly 'toasted'.

4. Serve warm or cold.

Gremolata Topping

Sprinkle this fresh-tasting mixture over casseroles and roasts just before serving – it's particularly good on lamb, chicken and beans.

1. Chop a handful of fresh parsley, crush two or three garlic cloves and finely grate the rind from a large lemon.

2. Mix the three ingredients together and there you have it!

Cheese and Walnut Toasts

Delicious appetisers with a whopping flavour 'hit'. Eat as a snack or top with just one of the cheeses and use as a topping for hotpots, casseroles or stew; add and cook uncovered for the final 10–15 minutes. Or float them on soup in flameproof dishes and flash under a hot grill to melt the cheese. Try making them with different breads too – sun-dried tomato, olive, nut or herb and garlic.

Serves 6–8

1 long French stick
2 garlic cloves
85g/3 oz walnuts
100g/3½ oz Double Gloucester cheese
100g/3½ oz halloumi cheese
150ml/¼ pint passata (sieved tomatoes)
2 tbsp tomato purée
Freshly milled black pepper
Small handful oregano leaves
Olive oil

1. Preheat the oven to 200°C, Fan 185°C, Gas 6.

2. Slice the French stick diagonally into 12–18 thin slices.

3. Crush the garlic cloves and roughly chop the walnuts. Coarsely grate the Double Gloucester cheese and finely chop the halloumi cheese.

4. Put the garlic in a bowl and stir in the passata, tomato purée and a little black pepper. In another bowl mix the two cheeses with the walnuts and oregano leaves.

5. Spread the bread slices on one side with a thin layer of the tomato mixture, taking it right up to the edges. Pile the cheese mixture on top.

6. Arrange in a single layer on baking sheets and drizzle with a little olive oil. Put into the hot oven and cook for about 12–15 minutes until golden, crisp and piping hot.

7. Serve hot or warm.

Pesto

This classic Italian sauce needs no cooking. Stir it into freshly cooked pasta, spread it on toasted bread, spoon it over vegetables, or add a spoonful to a bowl of soup. To make a winter version, use parsley in place of basil and walnuts instead of pine nuts. Lightly toasting the nuts first (in the oven, under the grill or in a dry frying pan) adds a lovely flavour. To make the pesto, use a stick blender, a processor or large pestle and mortar. Once made, keep pesto in the fridge – so long as the surface is covered with olive oil, it should keep for 2–3 weeks.

Serves 4–6

1 small garlic clove
50g/1¾ oz Parmesan cheese
About 1 handful of pine nuts
About 3 handfuls of fresh basil leaves
About 200ml/7 fl oz extra virgin olive oil
Freshly milled black pepper

1. Chop the garlic and cut the cheese into small pieces. Using a stick blender, processor or pestle and mortar, grind the cheese with the garlic, pine nuts, basil (you may need to add this in batches) and a little olive oil until finely chopped.

2. Season with black pepper and, still mixing and grinding, slowly add the oil to make a thick, soft paste.

3. Chill until required (see note above).

Flavoured Butters

Useful to keep in the fridge. Can be wrapped in waxed paper, then rolled into a sausage shape and chilled. Slice to put on top of steaks, both meat and fish. Or spread on breads or wraps. Sweet butters are best made with unsalted butter and are delicious on pancakes, hot-cooked fruits or sweet tarts.

Makes about 100g/3½ oz

100g/3½ oz salted or unsalted butter
Freshly milled salt and pepper or a little clear honey
Your favourite savoury or sweet additions (see below)

1. Put the butter in a small bowl and mix until soft and creamy (or soften it in the microwave on a low power level).

2. Slowly beat in the ingredients of your choice and season or sweeten if necessary.

3. Spoon into small dishes, cover and chill. Alternatively spoon the flavoured butter onto baking paper and roll up into a sausage shape. Twist the ends of the paper (like a Christmas cracker), chill and slice off pieces as required.

Savoury Variations:

Herb
2 tbsp freshly chopped parsley and 1 tbsp freshly chopped chives

Rosemary
1 tsp freshly chopped rosemary leaves

Garlic
1 crushed garlic clove and 1 tsp lemon juice

Olive & Oregano
3 chopped pitted black olives and 1 tbsp freshly chopped oregano leaves

Curry & Ginger
¼ tsp ground ginger and ½ tsp grated root ginger

Sweet Variations:

Orange & Walnut
1 tsp grated orange rind and 2 tbsp chopped walnuts

Lemon & Ginger
1 tsp grated lemon rind and ¼ tsp ground ginger

Cranberry & Orange
1 tbsp dried ready-to-eat cranberries and 1 tsp grated orange
rind

Raspberry Vermouth
6–8 crushed raspberries and 1 tbsp sweet red vermouth

Marmalade & Whisky
1 tbsp marmalade and 1 tbsp whisky

Hot Garlic Bread

Though we use a French stick, garlic bread can be made with loaves of all shapes and sizes. Soften fridge-hard butter in the microwave on a low power.

Serves 8–10

4 garlic cloves
100g/3½ oz soft butter
1 large French stick

1. Preheat the oven to 200°C, Fan 185°C, Gas 6.

2. Crush or finely chop the garlic and stir into the soft butter until evenly mixed.

3. With a bread knife, make diagonal cuts into the bread, about 2.5cm/1 inch apart, without slicing through the bottom crust (so the loaf doesn't fall apart).

4. Spread the garlic butter between the slices. Any extra can be scraped over the top of the loaf. Wrap the loaf loosely in a large sheet of foil.

5. Put the foil-wrapped loaf into the hot oven and cook for 10–15 minutes until the butter has melted through the bread and the crust is crisp and browned.

Hot Herb Bread

Follow the recipe for Hot Garlic Bread above, replacing the garlic with 2–4 tbsp freshly chopped herbs – parsley, thyme, chives, coriander, or a mixture. A little finely-grated lemon rind adds a nice freshness too.

Soda Bread

Soda bread is best served warm on the day it is made, or toasted the day after. It's particularly good with soups and casseroles. Instead of buttermilk you could use half natural yogurt (the plain sort) and half water. To make a cheese version, add about 100g/3½ oz grated mature cheese at the end of step 2 and, just before cooking (at the end of step 4), sprinkle the shaped dough with a little extra cheese.

Makes 4 wedges

450g/1 lb plain white flour, plus extra for dusting
1 tbsp baking powder
1 tsp bicarbonate of soda
1 tsp salt
50g/1¾ oz butter
284ml carton buttermilk

1. Put a baking sheet into the oven and preheat to 220°C, Fan 205°C, Gas 7.

2. Sift the flour, baking powder, bicarbonate of soda and salt into a large mixing bowl. Using your fingertips, rub in the butter until the mixture resembles coarse crumbs.

3. With a flat-end knife, stir the buttermilk into the flour mixture, gathering it together to make a soft dough (if the dough is too stiff, add a little cold water). Tip the dough onto a lightly floured surface and gently fold and stretch it until smooth. Shape into a ball and press the top down to flatten it slightly.

4. Put the dough onto the hot baking sheet and sift a little flour over the top. With a sharp knife, cut a deep cross in the top, but don't cut all the way through.

5. Put into the hot oven and cook for about 30 minutes or until well risen and the crust is golden brown. To check it's done, carefully turn the loaf over and tap the bottom – it should sound hollow when the bread is cooked; if not, return it to the oven for a few minutes more.

6. Leave to cool for at least 15 minutes before breaking into four wedges and serving.

Herb Scone Wedges

Warm scones, straight from the oven, are delicious served alongside a bowl of soup or casserole. To make cheese scones, add 50g/1¾ oz finely grated mature Cheddar cheese and ¾ tsp mustard powder at the end of step 2 (either leave the herbs in too, or omit them, as you please). Add a glossy golden glaze by brushing the scones with beaten egg instead of milk in step 5.

Makes 8 wedges

225g/8 oz self-raising flour, plus extra
1 tsp baking powder
50g/1¾ oz butter
2 tbsp freshly chopped herbs, such as parsley, chives, thyme (or a mixture)
1 medium egg
About 5 tbsp milk, plus extra for brushing

1. Preheat the oven to 220°C, Fan 205°C, Gas 7.

2. Into a large bowl, sift the flour and baking powder. Cut the butter into small cubes and add to the flour. Using your fingertips, rub the butter into the flour until the mixture resembles fine crumbs. Stir in the herbs.

3. Lightly beat the egg and, with a round-end knife, mix in sufficient milk to make a soft dough. Tip out onto a lightly floured surface and gently fold and stretch it until smooth.

4. Pat or roll the dough into a rough circle about 1cm/½ inch thick. With a sharp knife, cut into eight wedges.

5. Lightly dust a baking sheet with flour and arrange the wedges (still in a circle) on it. Brush the tops lightly with milk.

6. Put into the hot oven and cook for about 12 minutes or until well risen and golden brown.

7. Leave to cool on a wire rack and serve warm or at room temperature.

Parmesan, Parsley and Mustard Muffins

Savoury mini muffins are delicious eaten warm. Or serve with soups, omelettes, drinks, or in place of rice or potatoes. You will need a 12-hole mini-muffin tin and paper cases.

Makes 12

300g/10½ oz self-raising flour
1 tsp baking powder
2 medium eggs
4 tbsp olive oil
250ml/9 fl oz milk
60g/2¼ oz grated Parmesan cheese
2 tbsp wholegrain mustard
2 tbsp chopped fresh parsley

1. Preheat the oven to 200°C, Fan 185°C, Gas 6.

2. Sift the flour and baking powder into a large bowl. Break the eggs into the flour and add the oil, milk, cheese, mustard and parsley.

3. With a wooden spoon, lightly beat the ingredients together until they are only just mixed (don't worry if the mixture is still a little lumpy – it's important not to over-mix). Spoon into the muffin cases.

4. Put into the hot oven and cook for 12–18 minutes until risen and firm to the touch. Turn out onto a cooling rack.

Chocolate Chunk and Almond Cookies

Serve these delicious cookies alongside desserts of fruit, ice cream, yogurt and so on. We have used dark chocolate and almonds, though they taste equally good with milk chocolate and walnuts, white chocolate and hazelnuts, or dark chocolate and pistachios. Just remember to chop the nuts roughly first.

Makes about 20

1 medium egg
½ tsp vanilla extract
150g/5½ oz self-raising flour
115g/4 oz dark chocolate
115g/4 oz soft butter
75g/2¾ oz caster sugar
75g/2¾ oz light muscovado sugar
60g/2¼ oz toasted flaked almonds

1. Preheat the oven to 180°C, Fan 165°C, Gas 4.

2. Lightly beat the egg with the vanilla extract. Sift the flour. Chop the chocolate into small chunks.

3. In a large mixing bowl, beat the butter and sugars together until soft, light and fluffy.

4. Gradually beat the egg into the butter mixture.

5. Mix in the flour, half at a time, then stir in the chocolate and nuts.

6. Put spoonfuls of the mixture onto baking sheets lined with baking paper, leaving plenty of room for the cookies to spread.

7. Put into the hot oven and cook for 10–12 minutes until light golden brown.

8. Leave to cool on the tray for a minute or two, and then transfer to a wire rack to cool completely.

Oven Rice

Cooking rice successfully in the oven depends on the rice absorbing all the liquid as it becomes tender, needing only a quick fluffing up with a fork before serving. The rice can be cooked in water or stock with or without added spices or herbs.

Serves 4 as an accompaniment

250g/9 oz long grain rice, such as white or easy-cook, white or brown basmati, fragrant or jasmine, or wild rice

1. Preheat the oven to 180°C, Fan 165°C, Gas 4.

2. Check with the packet instructions and, if necessary, rinse the rice.

3. Put the (drained) rice into a 1.7 litre/3 pint ovenproof casserole and stir in 500ml/18 fl oz boiling water (from the kettle).

4. Cover, put into the hot oven and cook until the rice is tender and has absorbed all the liquid. Cooking times will depend on the rice and whether you prefer yours with a bite, soft or sticky.

Long Grain: White or Easy-Cook White	30–40 minutes
Long Grain: Brown or Easy-Cook Brown	50–60 minutes
Basmati: White or Easy-Cook	25–35 minutes
Basmati: Brown	40 minutes
Fragrant or Jasmine	20–25 minutes
Wild Rice	1¼-1½ hours

5. Fluff up with a fork before serving. If wished, stir in a little butter or olive oil.

Root Vegetable Crisps

Expensive to buy, but cheap and easy to make. We like to use chilli for a hot, spicy taste, but it is optional; for a change try a little curry powder, or ground coriander, or just black pepper. You will need 2–3 baking sheets and, as beetroots can stain, we always use disposable gloves when preparing them. Serve au naturel or with yogurt or mayonnaise for dunking.

Serves 6–8

2 medium carrots
1 medium parsnip
2 small turnips
2 medium potatoes
2 medium beetroots
2–3 tbsp vegetable oil
1 tsp ground chilli powder
Freshly milled sea salt and black pepper

1. Preheat the oven to 200°C, Fan 185°C, Gas 6.

2. Peel and very thinly slice all the vegetables.

3. Put the oil in a large bowl and mix in the chilli powder. Add the vegetable slices and carefully turn until thoroughly coated (you may find this easier to do in two batches).

4. Arrange in single layers on baking sheets. Put into the hot oven (in batches if necessary) and cook for 10–15 minutes or until crisp and golden. Drain on kitchen paper.

5. Season if necessary and serve hot or cold.

Spiced Seeds and Nuts

Nibble with drinks or as a snack, or coarsely chop and use as a nutty topping for pasta dishes or over vegetables. They can be stored in a jar or sealed container for a few days, or they will keep for a week if left to cool and kept in an airtight tin.

Serves 8–10

350g/12 oz shelled unsalted nuts, such as peanuts, macadamia, blanched almonds, pecans or walnuts
2 tbsp olive oil
2 tbsp wholegrain mustard
2 tbsp sweet chilli sauce
2 tsp paprika pepper
100g/3½ oz sesame seeds
100g/3½ oz pumpkin seeds
100g/3½ oz sunflower seeds

1. Preheat the oven to 190°C, Fan 175°C, Gas 5.

2. Leave the nuts whole or, if you prefer, cut larger ones such as brazils or macadamias in half.

3. In a large bowl, mix together the oil, mustard, chilli sauce and paprika. Add all the nuts and seeds and mix until well coated. Spread thinly over two or three baking sheets.

4. Put into the hot oven and cook for 10 minutes or until hot and lightly 'toasted'.

5. Serve warm or cold (see note above).

Red Pepper Salsa

Salsa is the Mexican word for 'sauce'. It can be a raw or cooked mixture, mild, hot or very hot, with herbs or spices. Serve as an accompaniment with hot beef or meat steaks and chops, grilled or fried or roasted fish fillets or burgers, wraps and as a dip.

Serves 4–6

3 red onions
1 garlic clove
2 large red peppers
2 red chillies (see page 8)
Small bunch of parsley
Small bunch of coriander
6 tomatoes
1 lime
3 tbsp olive oil
Freshly milled salt and pepper

1. Finely chop the onions and garlic. Halve the peppers and chillies, remove and discard the seeds and stalks, and chop finely. Chop the parsley and coriander.

2. Halve the tomatoes, with a small spoon scoop out the seeds and chop the tomato flesh finely. Grate the rind from the lime, cut in half and squeeze the juice.

3. In a medium bowl, mix well all the ingredients except the salt and pepper. Season if necessary.

4. Cover and chill for 1 hour to let the flavours develop before serving.

Sprouted Seeds and Grains

It's easy to sprout seeds and grains at home, but only use those sold especially for sprouting, not the ones for growing in the garden as they could have been sprayed with insecticides. You need a shallow container, such as a disposable foil one. An alternative method to the one below is to put the seeds in a clean jar, cover with a square of muslin and secure with an elastic band. Fill the jar with cold water through the muslin and shake out the excess. Repeat each day until they have grown. Cut as they sprout and add to salads. Store refrigerated for 2 days in a polythene food bag.

Makes a large handful from each tray

Seeds and grains for sprouting, such as mung or aduki beans, alfalfa seeds, radish seeds, lentils and soya beans

1. Put a shallow oblong foil container on a wooden chopping board and carefully punch a few drainage holes in the bottom with a sharp pointed knife.

2. Lay two sheets of kitchen paper in the base of the tray and spray with cold water until thoroughly wet. Scatter a few seeds over the damp kitchen paper to give just a very thin covering, and then dampen the seeds with water. Cover the container with a sheet of kitchen paper to keep out the light.

3. Put the tray on a plate (to catch any drips) near natural light, such as a window sill or work surface, and spray each day with cold water. When the seeds begin to germinate and sprout (1–3 days) remove the paper cover and continue watering lightly each day (the paper should not be allowed to dry completely).

4. When the sprouts are 5–10cm/2–4 inches tall, cut with scissors and use (see note above).

Melon and Chicory Salad

Melon tastes so refreshing in a salad. A little nut oil has been added to the dressing; use sparingly as the flavour is very intense. Good served with pork, duck or game.

Serves 4–6

1 small honeydew melon
1 cucumber
6 spring onions
1 bunch watercress
3 chicory heads
Large handful of small salad leaves, or any crisp lettuce
   leaves
2 tbsp olive oil
1 tsp nut oil
1 tbsp raspberry vinegar
2 tbsp wholegrain mustard
Freshly milled salt and pepper

1. Quarter the melon, scoop out the seeds and, with a small sharp knife, cut the flesh away from the skin and chop roughly. Halve the cucumber lengthways, scoop out the seeds and slice the flesh thinly. Slice the onions and roughly chop the watercress. Separate the chicory heads into leaves.

2. Put all the fruit and salad ingredients in a large bowl.

3. Put the oils, raspberry vinegar, mustard and seasoning into a small jug and, with a fork or whisk, mix well.

4. Drizzle the dressing over the salad and serve immediately.

8

SLOW PUDS

Puddings may be an indulgence, but for most of us they are one of life's essentials. Just dip into this section and see if you can resist. These glamorous desserts will round off a dinner to perfection, but you may not want to wait until evening to try the Fruity Clafouti, the Baked Vanilla Ricotta with Honey and Figs, or the Chocolate Fondant Cakes with a gooey centre. Then there's easy-to-make free-form Apple and Blackberry Pie and Spiced Plum Cobbler, or a twist on tradition, Baked Apples with Cinnamon and Ginger Crunch. And look out for some sweet surprises – a pudding which makes its own sauce (try the lemon version on page 121, or the chocolate version on page 122), and a lasagne made with fruit – if you don't believe it, look on page 119.

....'ello darlin'

s a u c y   l e m o n

Roasted Fruits with Raspberry and Vermouth Sauce

Roasted fruits become slightly caramelised on the edges. Serve with toasted slices of fruit bread and natural yogurt.

Serves 6–8

4 medium, red, eating apples
4 firm peaches
8 apricots
1 tbsp oil
1 tbsp clear honey
200g/7 oz raspberries
3 tbsp icing sugar
3 tbsp dry vermouth, optional

1. Preheat the oven to 200°C, Fan 185°C, Gas 6.

2. Quarter the apples, remove the cores and cut each piece into two wedges. Halve the peaches, remove the stones and cut each half into three wedges. Halve the apricots and remove stones.

3. In a large bowl, mix together the oil and honey. Add the prepared fruit and stir gently until the fruit is coated.

4. Arrange in a single layer in a shallow, ovenproof dish. Put in the hot oven and cook for 15 minutes until the fruits are just cooked and lightly browned at the edges.

5. Meanwhile, put the raspberries in a bowl and whizz with a stick blender, or crush with a fork, until smooth. Add the icing sugar, dry vermouth (if using) and 150ml/¼ pint boiling water, mixing thoroughly.

6. Lift the cooked fruit from the dish and keep warm. Pour the raspberry mixture into the dish and stir, mixing in any juices from the bottom of the dish. Return the dish to the hot oven and cook a further 10 minutes.

7. Serve the fruits in warmed bowls with the sauce spooned over.

Baked Apples with Cinnamon and Ginger Crunch

Bramley apples are perfect for baking – they soften and begin to collapse into a fluffy mound. Ginger adds a spark to this dish. Serve with custard or vanilla ice cream.

Serves 6

6 medium cooking apples, such as Bramley
60g/2¼ oz blanched hazelnuts
60g/2¼ oz crystallised ginger
2 tbsp currants
60g/2¼ oz golden demerara sugar
40g/1½ oz butter, melted
1 tsp ground cinnamon

1. Preheat the oven to 190°C, Fan 175°C, Gas 5.

2. With a corer or a small, sharp knife remove the apple cores. Score a line round the middle of each apple, cutting just through the skin.

3. Roughly chop the hazelnuts and finely chop the ginger. Put them in a medium bowl, add the currants, sugar, butter and cinnamon, and mix thoroughly.

4. With a small spoon push this mixture into the cavity of each apple, pressing down to pack as much in as possible.

5. Put the apples on a baking sheet and cook for about 35 minutes or until the apples are soft and starting to puff out of their skins but still hold their shape.

6. Serve hot or warm.

Slow-Cooked Fruits with Cinnamon

Put fresh and dried fruits in a dish with juice and honey, put in the oven and leave – simple and delicious. Packets of mixed dried fruits are readily available. Eat with porridge for breakfast or as a dessert with cream or yogurt.

Serves 6–8

2 red apples
2 medium seedless oranges
400g/14 oz mixed whole or sliced dried fruits such as prunes, apple slices, figs, apricots and pears
100g/3½ oz sultanas
4 tbsp clear honey
450ml/16 fl oz unsweetened apple juice
5cm/2 inch cinnamon stick

1. Quarter the apples, remove the cores and chop roughly. Leaving the peel on, thinly slice the oranges.

2. Put all the ingredients in a medium ovenproof dish, and stir until thoroughly mixed.

3. Cover, put in the oven and cook at 160°C, Fan 145°C, Gas 3 for 1½–2 hours until the fruits are cooked and very soft.

Mango, Banana and Fresh Coconut Crisp

The flavour of fresh coconut is an ideal match with mango and banana. To open a coconut, push a pointed screwdriver into the three 'eyes' at one end and pour out the liquid. Wrap the nut in a towel, put on a solid floor and hit gently with a hammer until it breaks. With a sharp knife cut the flesh from the shell.

Serves 6–8

¼ fresh coconut, or 100g/3½ oz desiccated coconut
2 large ripe mangos
3 bananas
1 large orange
300ml/½ pint apple juice
3 tbsp clear honey

1. Cut open the coconut (see note above) and coarsely grate the white flesh – you will need about 200g/7 oz.

2. Preheat the oven to 190°C, Fan 175°C, Gas 5.

3. Peel the mangos, slice the flesh from the stone and chop roughly. Peel and thickly slice the bananas. Grate the rind from the orange, cut in half and squeeze the juice.

4. Pour the apple juice into a medium jug and stir in the honey, orange rind and juice.

5. Mix the mangos, bananas and three-quarters of the coconut in a 1 litre/1¾ pint ovenproof dish. Pour over the liquid and scatter the remaining coconut over the top.

6. Cover, put in the oven and cook for 25–35 minutes until the fruits are soft and the top is crisp and golden.

Rustic Apple and Blackberry Pie

A free-form fruit pie that takes minutes to make. Raspberries, blackcurrants, whinberries or blueberries could be used in place of blackberries. Serve with thick yogurt, cream, custard or vanilla ice cream.

Serves 6

1 small lemon
500g/1 lb 2 oz eating apples
75g/2¾ oz caster sugar, plus 1 tbsp
¼ tsp mixed spice (optional)
250g/9 oz blackberries
375g packet ready-rolled shortcrust pastry

1. Preheat the oven to 200°C, Fan 185°C, Gas 6.

2. Halve the lemon and squeeze the juice. Cut the apples into quarters, remove the cores and cut the fruit into chunky pieces. Stir together 75g/2¾ oz sugar and the mixed spice (if using). Put the apples into a large bowl with the blackberries, lemon juice and sugar mixture. Toss together gently until the sugar has dissolved.

3. Unroll the pastry and lay it over a 25cm/10 inch ovenproof pie plate or shallow dish. Tip the fruit mixture into the centre. Fold the edges of the pastry up and over the fruit in a rough fashion and sprinkle the remaining 1 tbsp sugar over the top.

4. Put into the hot oven and cook for 30–40 minutes until the pastry is golden and the fruit is tender.

Spiced Plum Cobbler

It's so easy – simply spoon the quick-to-make topping over the fruit and bake! The cornflour helps to thicken the sauce around the fruit. Serve with crème fraîche, cream or custard.

Serves 6

900g/2 lb plums
150g/5½ oz caster sugar, plus 3 tbsp
1 tbsp cornflour
250g/9 oz self-raising flour
1 generous tsp mixed spice
100g/3½ oz chilled butter
175ml/6 fl oz buttermilk or whole natural yogurt

1. Preheat the oven to 200°C, Fan 185°C, Gas 6.

2. Halve the plums, remove the stones and cut the fruit into chunky pieces. Toss the plums with 3 tbsp caster sugar and the cornflour. Spread the mixture in a shallow oven-proof dish measuring about 25 x 17.5cm/10 x 7 inches.

3. Sift the flour and spice into a mixing bowl and stir in 100g/3½ oz sugar. Cut the butter into small cubes and add to the flour mixture. Using your fingertips, rub the butter into the flour until the mixture resembles fine crumbs (or do this part in a food processor). Stir in the buttermilk or yogurt until just combined – the resulting dough with be quite soft and sticky.

4. Arrange spoonfuls of the dough over the fruit – don't spread it evenly, leave some of the plums uncovered. Sprinkle the remaining sugar over the top.

5. Put into the hot oven and cook for 30–40 minutes until the topping is golden and the plums are soft.

Fruity Clafouti

As well as plums, this works well with whole cherries or wedges of ripe peaches or apricots. Serve the pudding warm, dusted with icing sugar and a jug of pouring cream alongside.

Serves 4–6

500g/1 lb 2 oz plums
115g/4 oz caster sugar
125g/4½ oz plain flour
Pinch of salt
3 medium eggs
400ml/14 fl oz milk
Butter
Icing sugar, to serve

1. Halve the plums and remove the stones. Toss the plums with half the sugar and, if time allows, leave to stand for about 30 minutes.

2. Meanwhile, sift the flour and salt into a mixing bowl and stir in the remaining sugar. Make a well in the centre and break the eggs into it. Gradually beat the flour into the eggs, adding the milk to make a smooth batter. Cover and leave to stand until required, stirring well before using.

3. Preheat the oven to 180°C, Fan 165°C, Gas 4.

4. Butter a shallow ovenproof dish (large enough to hold the fruit in a single layer), scatter the plums in it and pour the batter over.

5. Put the dish into the hot oven and cook for about 30 minutes or until the batter is puffed up and cooked through.

6. Serve immediately with a little icing sugar sifted over.

Fruit Lasagne

What a surprise! Lasagne made with fruit, not with minced meat. Pasta has a neutral flavour so can be used in sweet dishes as well as savoury. We used fresh lasagne sheets so that we could cut it with scissors in order to fit the dish, but the dried variety works just as well.

Serves 4–6

Butter, for greasing
2 large cooking apples, such as Bramley
8 plums
2 limes
150ml/¼ pint orange juice
200g/7 oz sultanas
2 medium eggs
200g/7 oz mascarpone cheese
400ml/14 fl oz milk
2 tbsp clear honey
½ tsp ground cinnamon
½ tsp ground nutmeg
6–8 fresh lasagne sheets
2 tbsp demerara sugar

1. Preheat the oven to 180°C, Fan 165°C, Gas 4. Butter a 1.2 litre/2 pint ovenproof oval or oblong dish.
2. Peel and quarter the apples, remove the cores and slice the fruit thinly. Halve the plums and remove the stones. Finely grate the rind from the limes, cut in half and squeeze the juice.
3. In a large bowl, mix together the orange juice, sultanas, apples, plums, lime rind and juice.
4. Break the eggs into a large jug and stir in the mascarpone, milk, honey, cinnamon and nutmeg, mixing until smooth.
5. Spoon some of the fruit mixture into the dish and cover with a single layer of pasta sheets (if necessary cut them to fit). Pour over a little of the egg mixture. Continue with the layers, ending with pasta and pouring over the remaining liquid. Sprinkle the sugar over the top.
6. Put into the hot oven and cook for 45 minutes until the pasta is soft and golden on top.
7. Cut and serve immediately.

Baked Vanilla Ricotta with Honey and Figs

Vary the fruit according to season – juicy, ripe peaches or pears are good, or try soft fruits such as strawberries, raspberries and blackberries.

Serves 6

Oil
2 eggs
Three 250g cartons ricotta
4 tbsp soft brown sugar
2 vanilla pods
About 9 fresh ripe figs
Runny honey

1. Lightly oil six small ovenproof dishes or moulds.

2. Preheat the oven to 180°C, Fan 165°C, Gas 4.

3. Lightly beat the eggs in a large mixing bowl. Add the ricotta and sugar and, using a whisk, beat until smooth.

4. Slit the vanilla pods lengthways (with the tip of a sharp knife), scrape out the tiny black seeds and stir them into the ricotta mixture.

5. Spoon the mixture into the prepared dishes and put onto a baking sheet.

6. Put into the hot oven and cook for 35–40 minutes until risen and golden brown on top.

7. Meanwhile, cut the figs into halves or quarters and drizzle with honey to taste.

8. Serve the puddings warm with the fruit and honey.

Saucy Lemon Pudding

A well-known traditional favourite. It's always a surprise when the pudding is cooked; it produces a light lemon sponge on top of a delicious lemon sauce. Serve with custard or natural yogurt.

Serves 4

Butter, for greasing
2 large lemons
1 tbsp self-raising flour
3 medium eggs
90g/3¼ oz caster sugar
200ml/7 fl oz milk
Pinch of salt
1 tbsp icing sugar

1. Preheat the oven to 180°C, Fan 165°C, Gas 4. Lightly butter a 1 litre/1¾ pint ovenproof dish.

2. Finely grate the rind from the lemons, cut in half and squeeze the juice. Sift the flour into a small bowl. Break the eggs, separating the yolks and whites into two large bowls.

3. To the egg yolks, add the sugar and whisk or beat until creamy, fluffy and pale. Whisk in the milk, flour, lemon juice and lemon rind until thoroughly mixed.

4. To the egg whites, add the salt and (with a clean whisk) beat until stiff but not dry, gradually adding the icing sugar as you mix.

5. With a large metal spoon and using a cutting action, carefully fold the egg white mixture into the lemon mixture until both are thoroughly combined. Pour the mixture into the prepared dish.

6. Stand the dish in a roasting tin and add sufficient hot water to come half way up the sides of the dish. Put in the hot oven and cook for 1 hour or until the sponge is cooked (it will feel softly firm to the touch) and pale golden brown.

7. Serve whilst hot.

Saucy Chocolate Pudding

And here's a chocolate pudding that comes with its own sauce. The method differs from that of Saucy Lemon Pudding on page 121. During cooking, the sauce that is poured over the pudding mixture sinks to the bottom, while the chocolate sponge rises to the top. It's lovely served with a spoonful or two of crème fraîche.

Serves 6

150g/5½ oz soft butter or margarine, plus extra for
  greasing
150g/5½ oz self-raising flour
6 tbsp cocoa
150g/5½ oz caster sugar
3 medium eggs
2 tbsp milk
1 tsp vanilla extract
150g/5½ oz muscovado sugar

1. Lightly butter a 1.7 litre/3 pint ovenproof dish. Preheat the oven to 190°C, Fan 175°C, Gas 5.

2. Sift the flour and 3 tbsp cocoa into a mixing bowl and add the butter or margarine and caster sugar. Break the eggs into a jug and beat in the milk and vanilla. Pour the egg mixture into the flour. Beat until well mixed, soft and smooth.

3. Spoon the mixture evenly into the buttered dish, gently levelling the surface.

4. In a jug or bowl mix the muscovado sugar with the remaining 3 tbsp cocoa. Stir in 350ml/12 fl oz hot water, stirring until smooth. Pour the hot sauce over the pudding mixture in the dish.

5. Put into the hot oven and cook for about 50 minutes until the sponge has risen to the top and is softly firm to the touch.

6. Serve hot or warm.

Chocolate Fondant Cakes

Catch them at the right stage and they will have soft centres of molten chocolate. They are ideal for making up to two days before you need them – in fact the mixture benefits from being allowed to set before cooking (see step 4). Serve with cream or yogurt.

Serves 4

115g/4 oz soft butter, plus extra for greasing
2 tsp plain flour, plus extra for dusting
175g/6 oz dark chocolate (with at least 50% cocoa solids)
2 medium eggs
2 medium egg yolks
60g/2¼ oz caster sugar

1. Lightly butter four ovenproof moulds or dishes. Add a little flour to each, shaking it round to coat the butter and tipping out any excess.

2. Break the chocolate into a bowl, add the butter and place on a pan of gently simmering water, stirring occasionally, until melted (don't allow the bowl to touch the water). Alternatively, heat in the microwave on medium power, stirring occasionally, until melted.

3. In a large mixing bowl, whisk the eggs and egg yolks with the sugar until the mixture is pale and thick. Quickly beat the melted chocolate into the egg mixture then, with a metal spoon and a cutting action, fold in the 2 tsp flour until well mixed.

4. Spoon the mixture into the prepared moulds and leave to stand in the refrigerator for at least 30 minutes and preferably several hours (see note above).

5. Preheat the oven to 230°C, Fan 215°C, Gas 8.

6. Stand the chilled moulds on a baking sheet, put into the hot oven and cook for 6–7 minutes until puffed up.

7. Leave to stand for 30–40 seconds before carefully sliding a knife round the edges to loosen them. Turn the puddings onto warmed plates and serve immediately.

INDEX

By the same authors

FRESH & FAST:
MEALS FROM THE HOB

With a hundred delicious and varied recipes, all quick and easy to make, you will amaze yourself with what you can achieve when time is tight.

Just spend a few minutes assembling easily purchased fresh produce and store-cupboard ingredients. Quickly cook on the hob, or maybe under the grill, and food can be on the table in the time it takes to heat a ready meal.

What a difference! Make your selection of fresh ingredients to conjure up, in next to no time, an appetising choice of dishes for all occasions. Annette Yates and Norma Miller accompany their recipes with plenty of serving suggestions and hints and tips to make things even easier.

Uniform with this book